I0443566

How to Draw Flowers and Trees

Sophia Williams

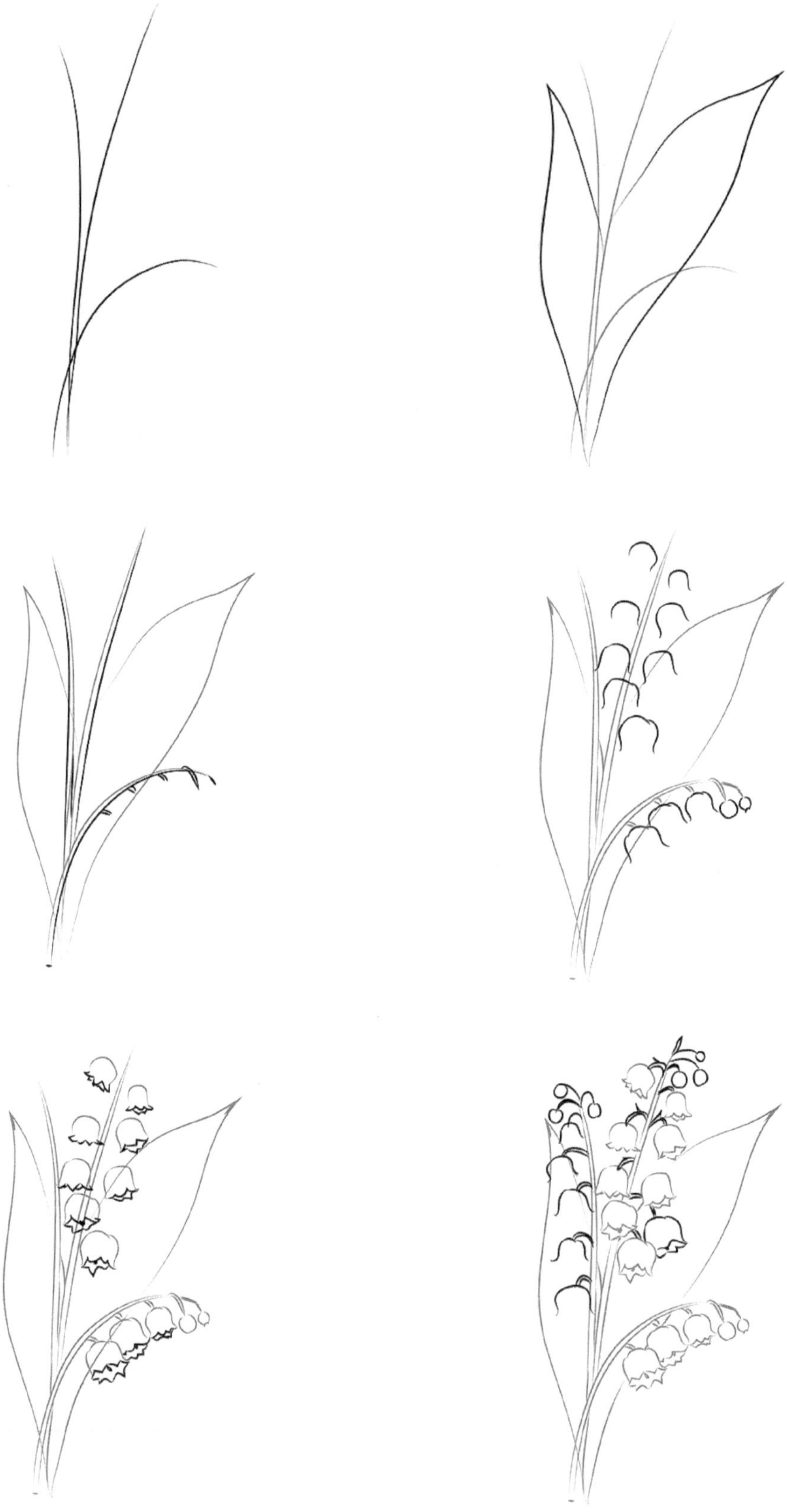

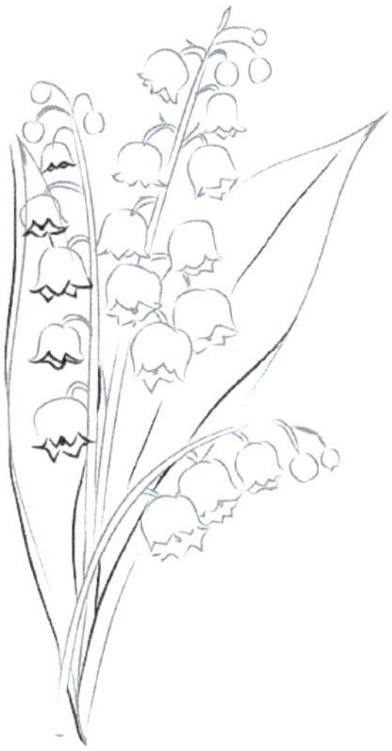
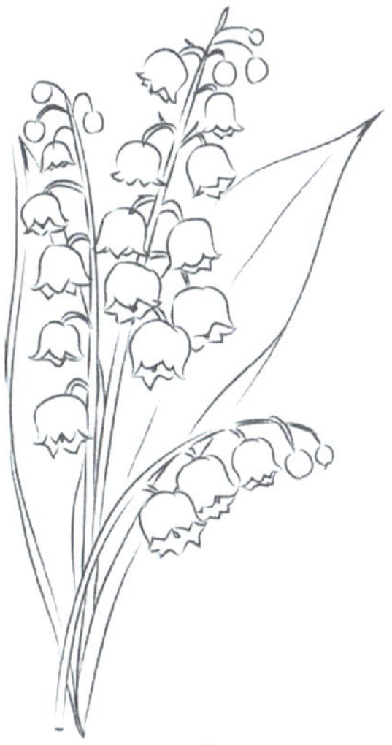
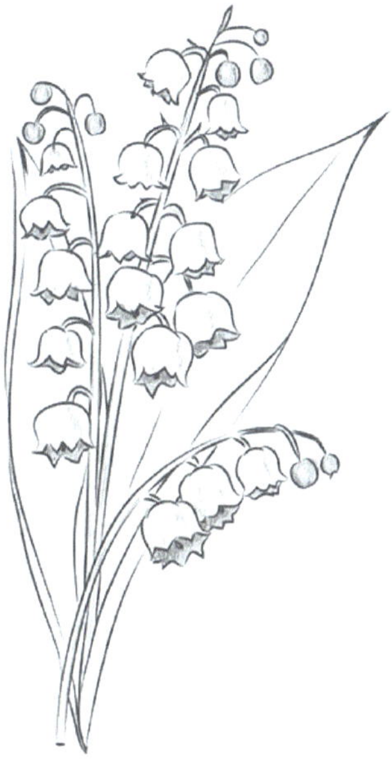
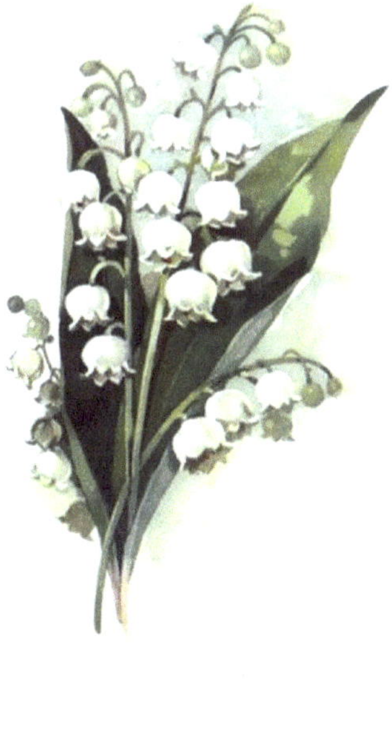

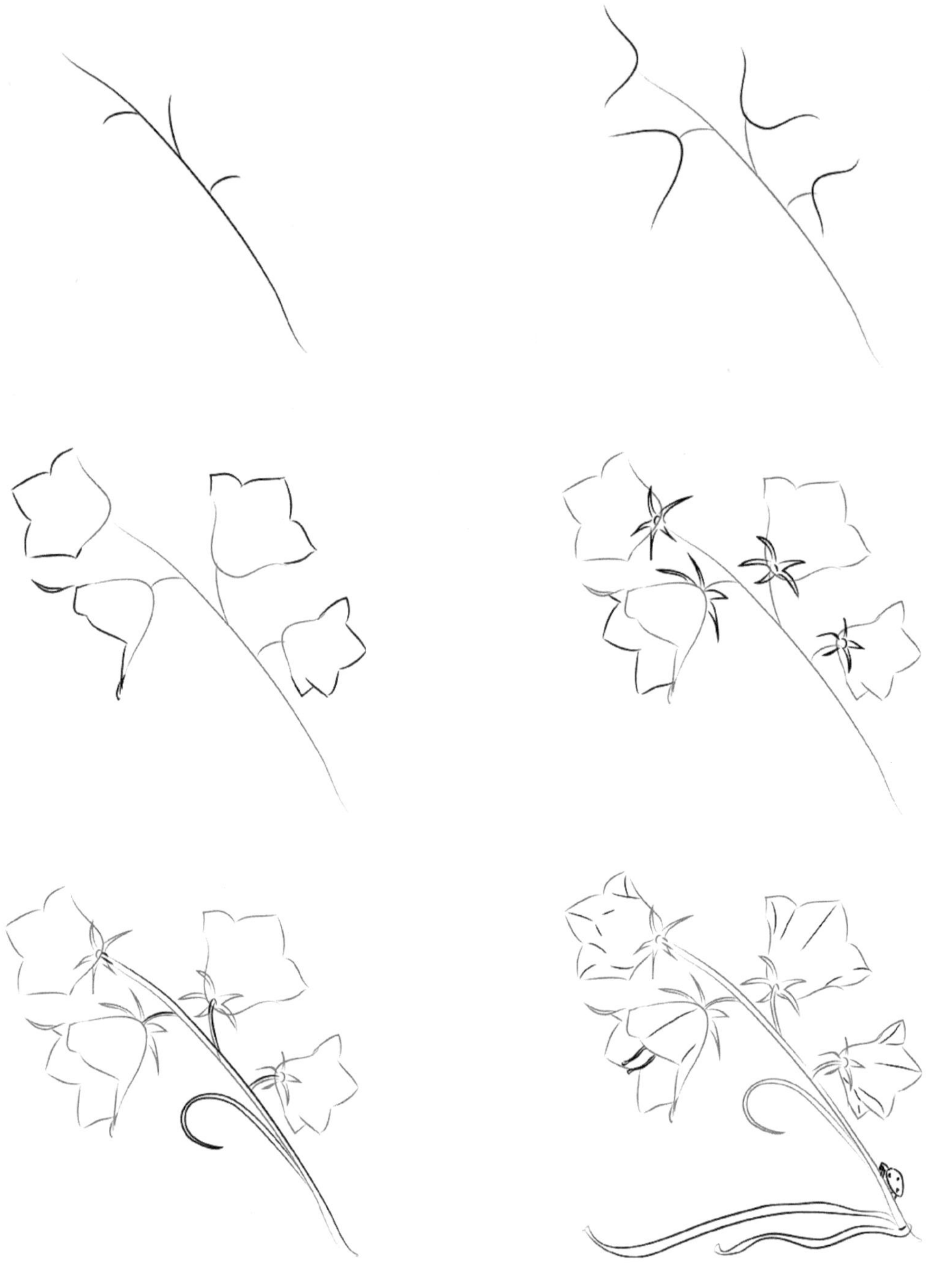

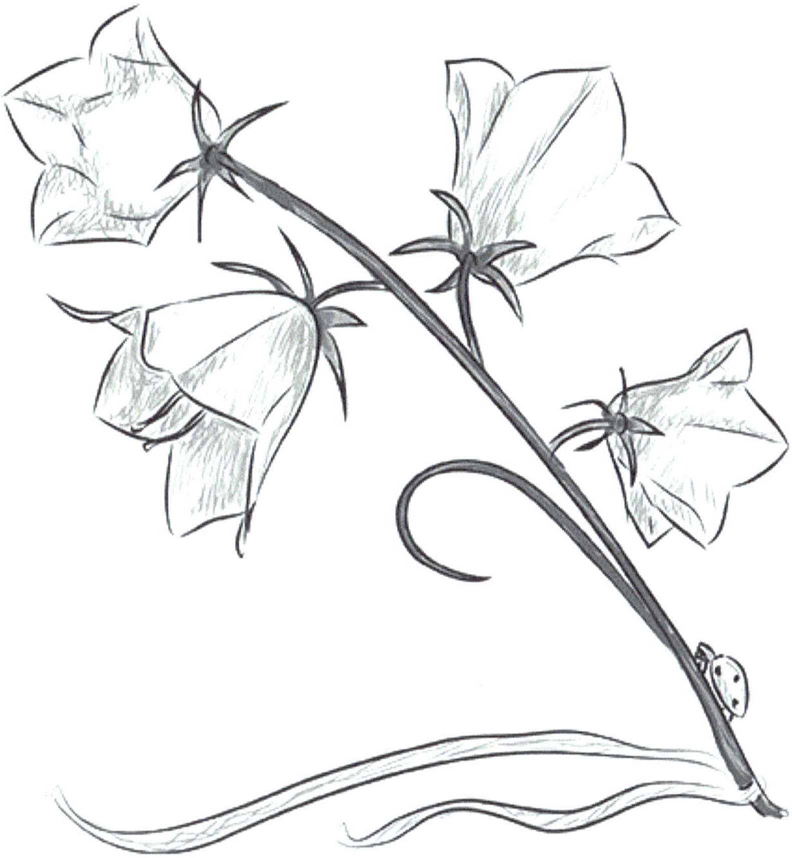

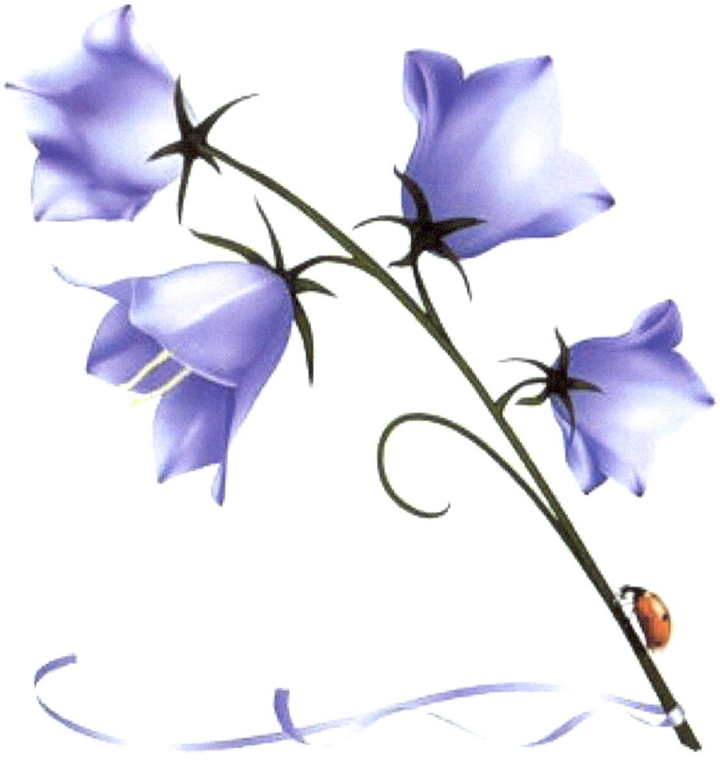

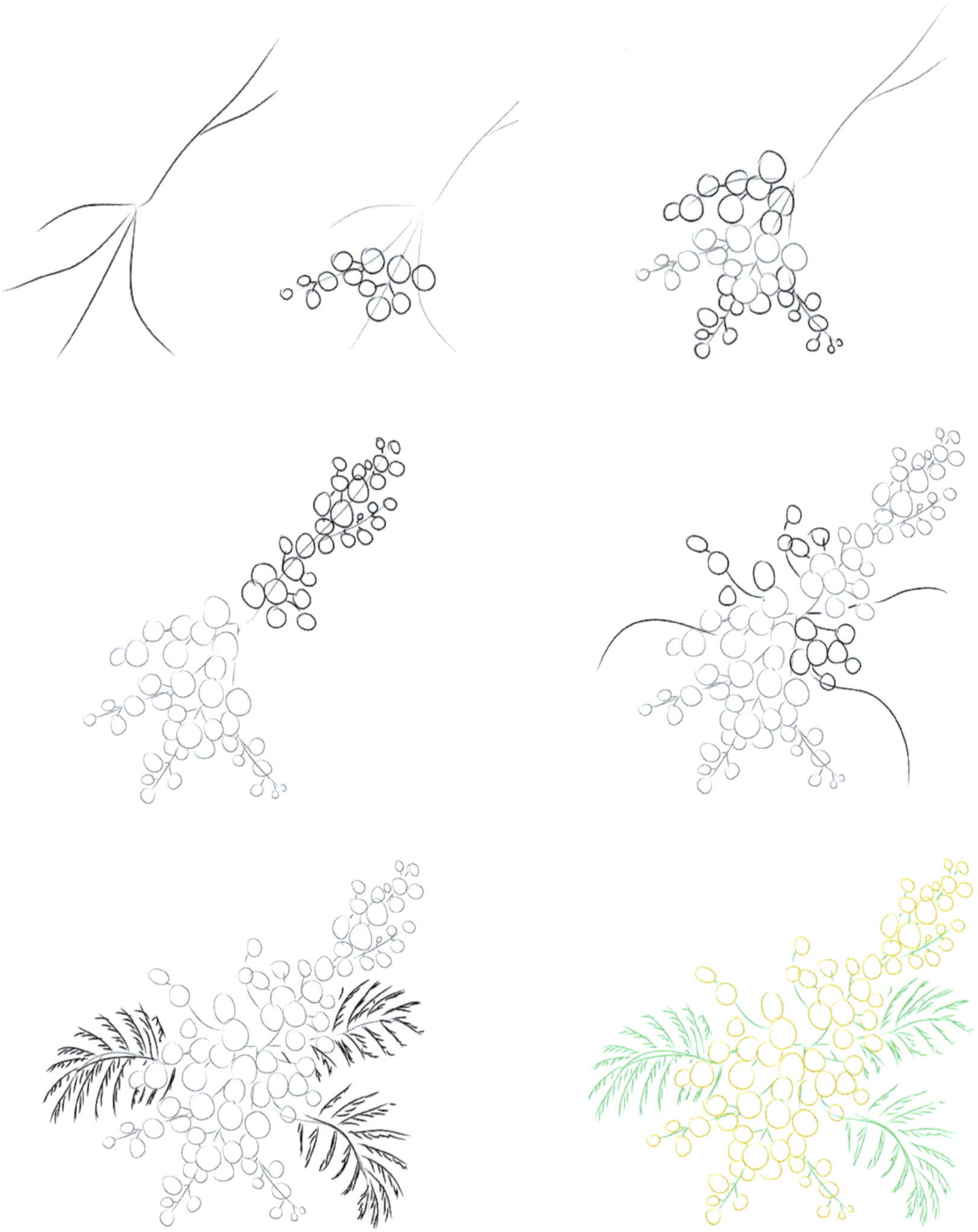

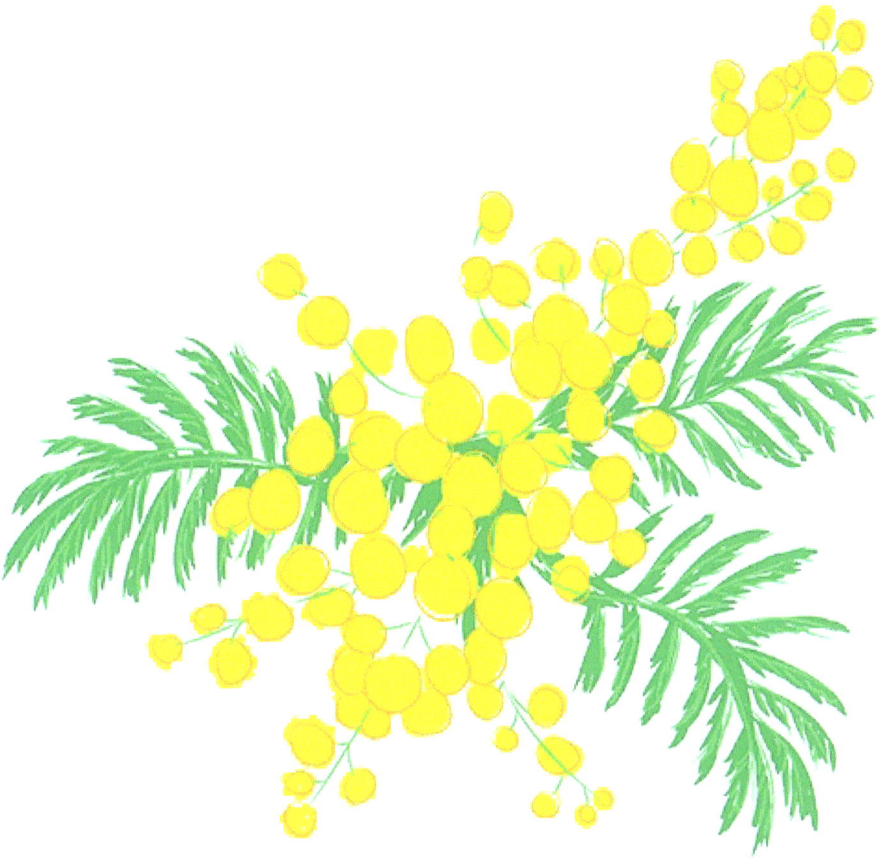

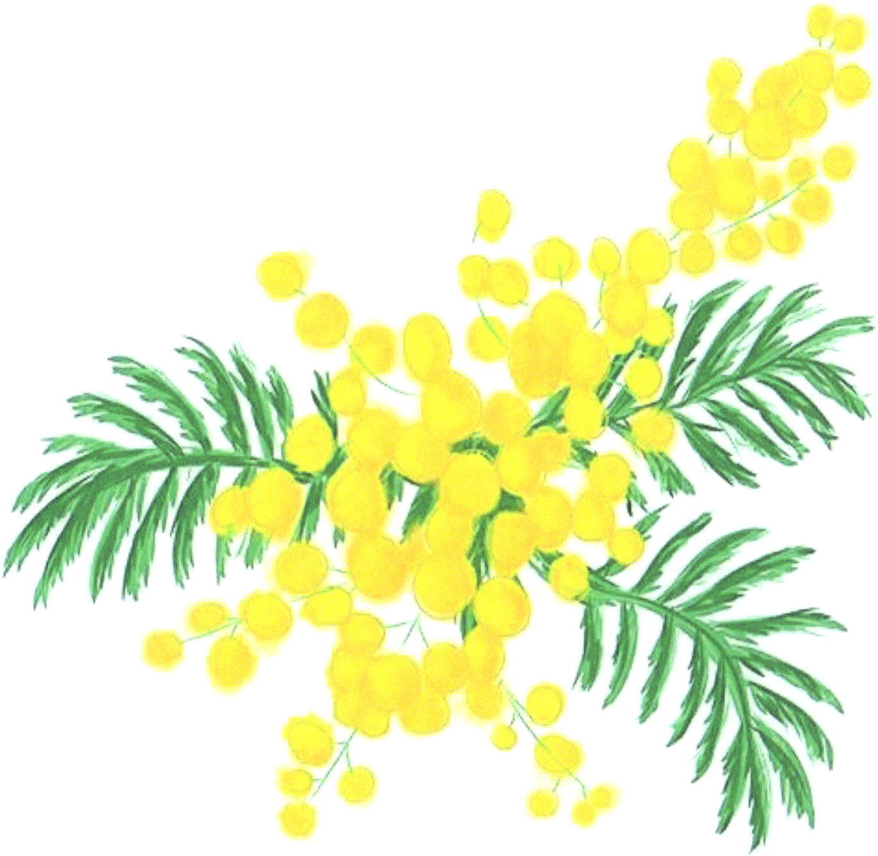

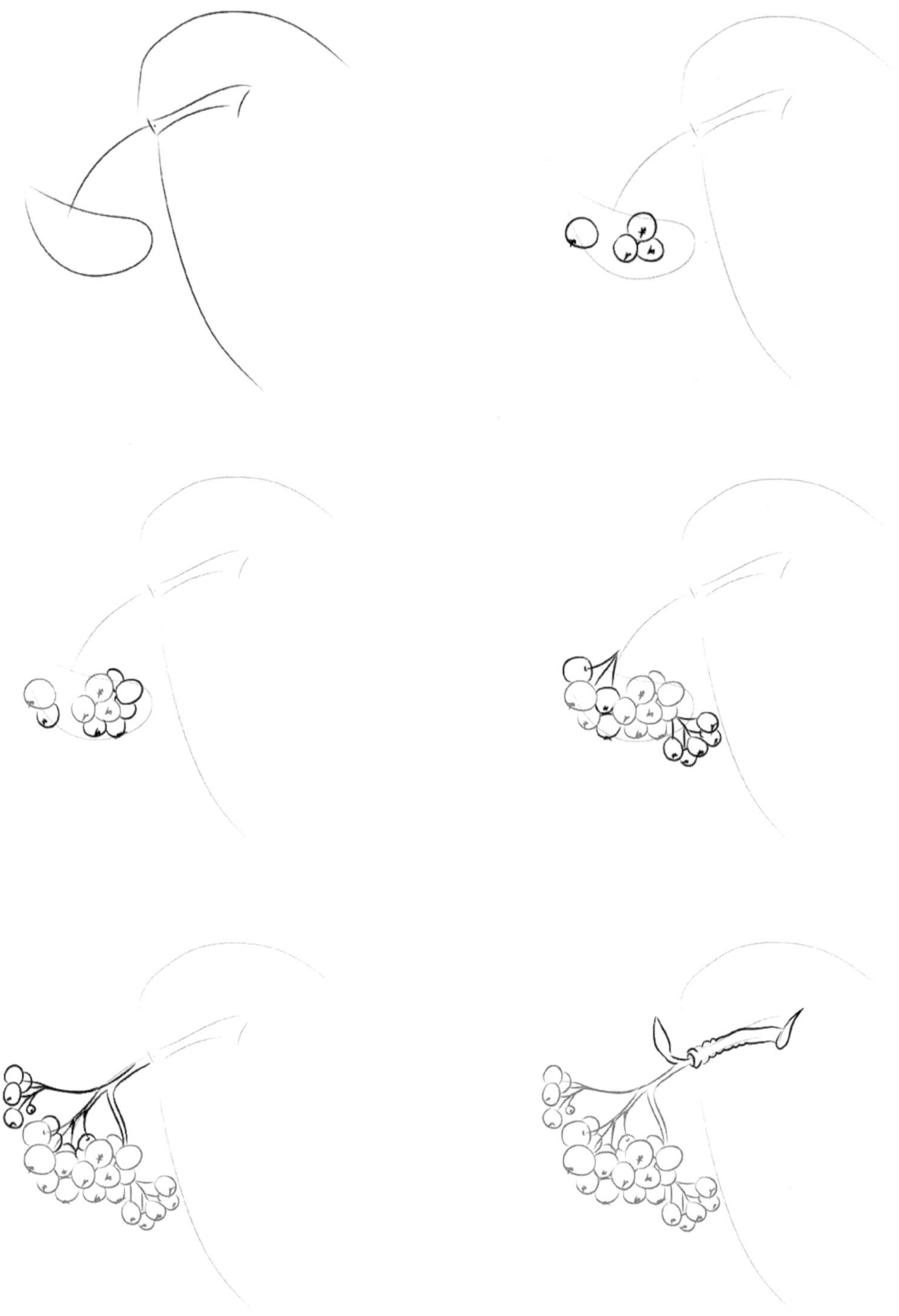

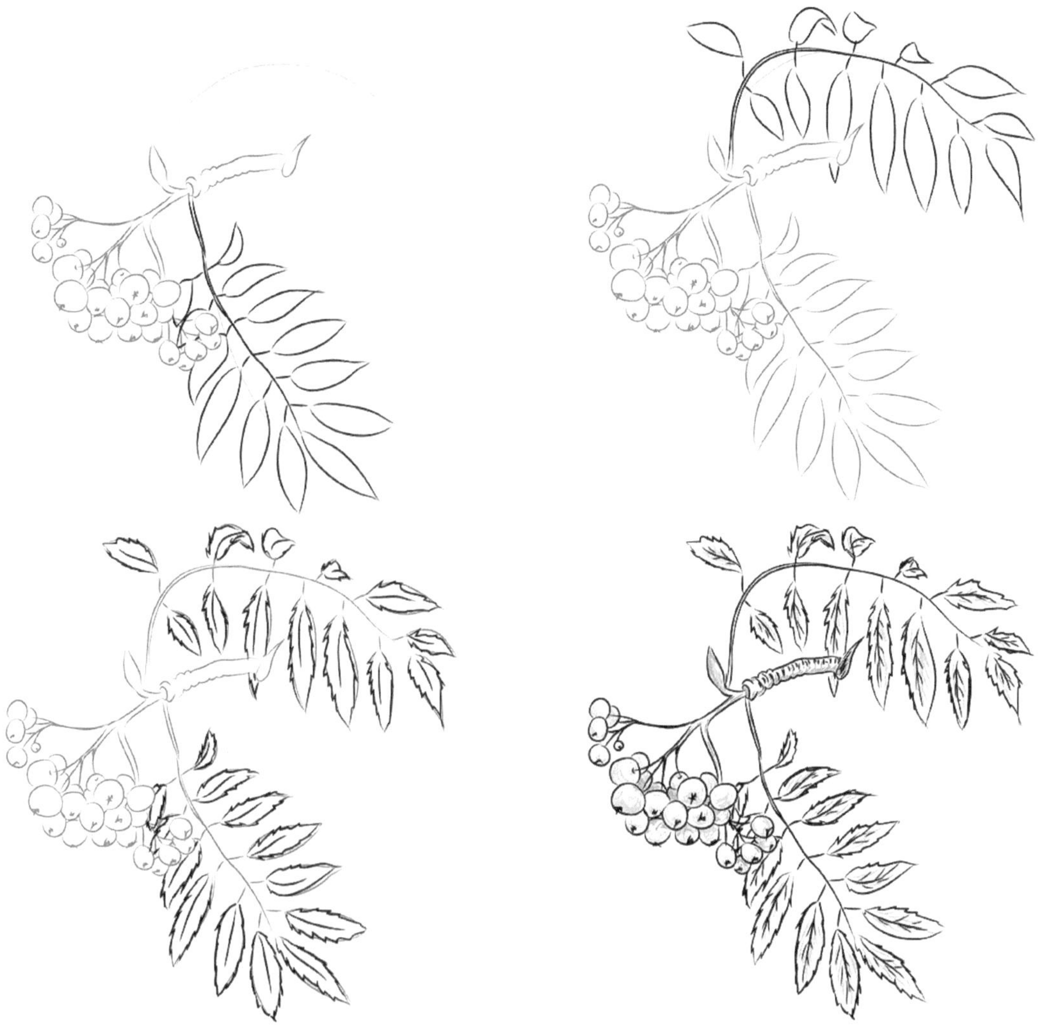

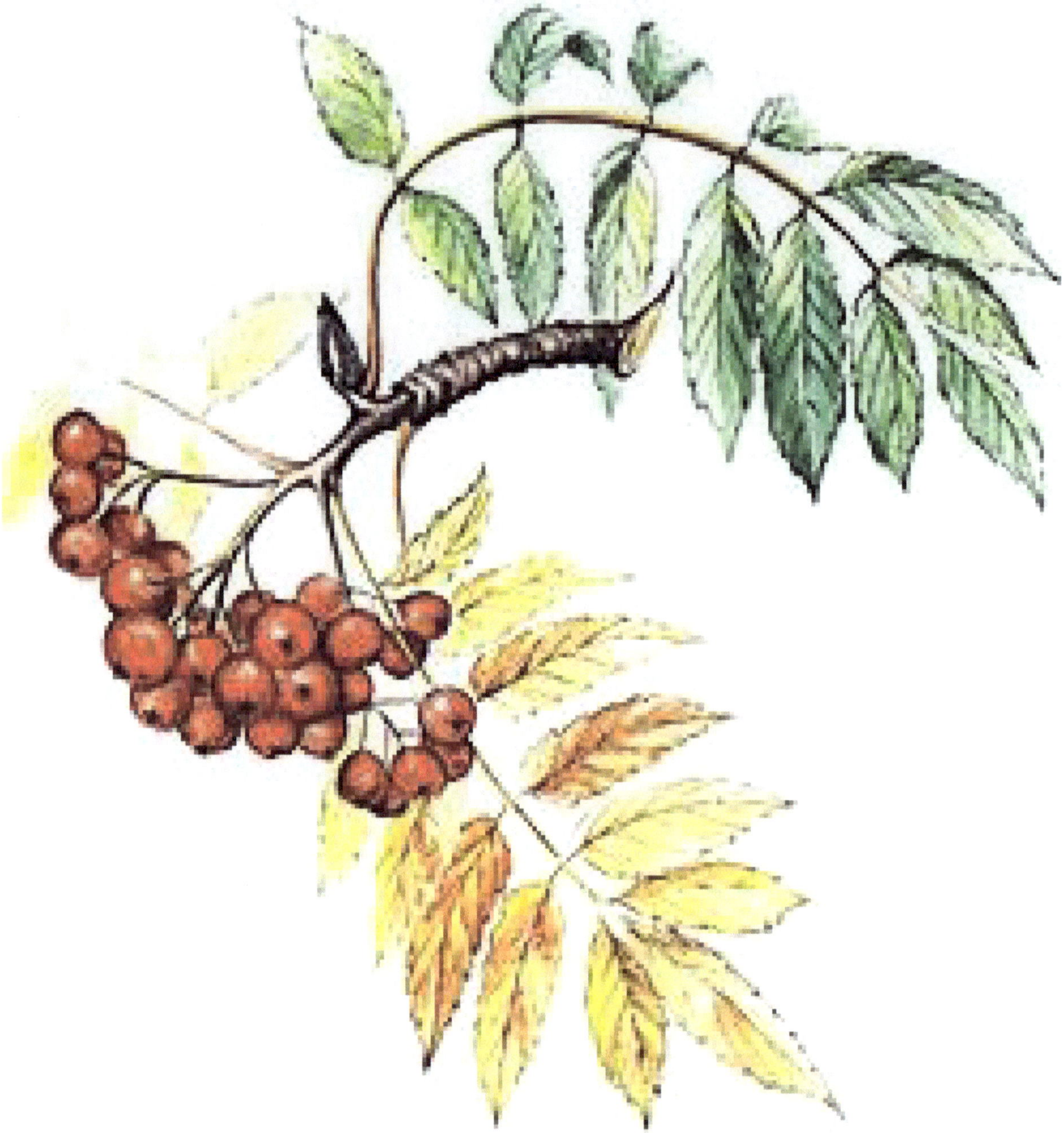

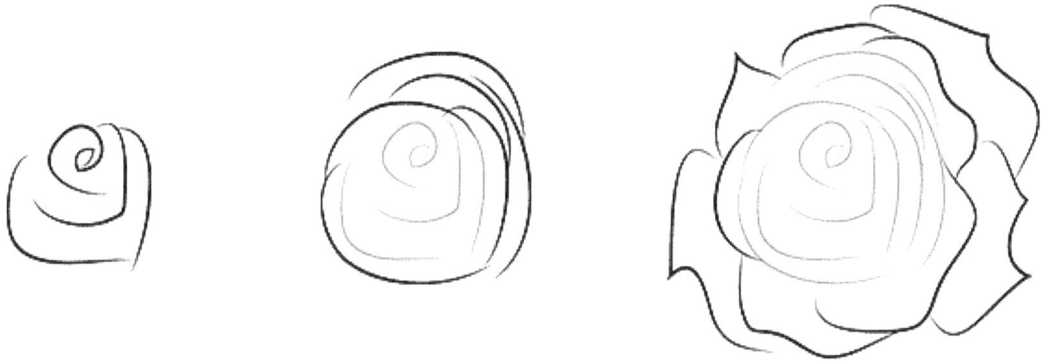

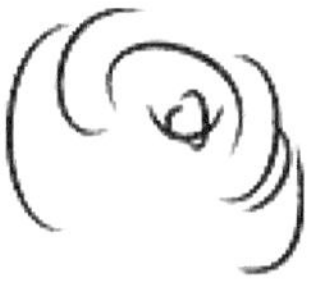

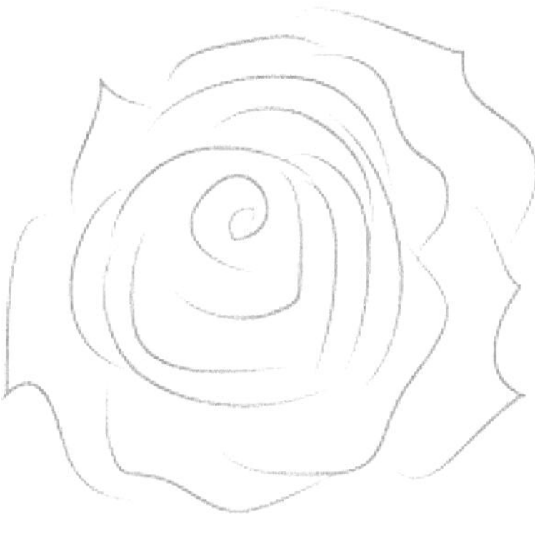

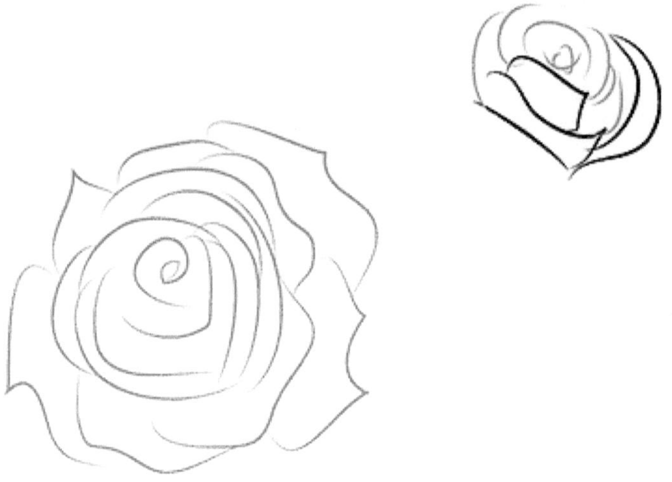

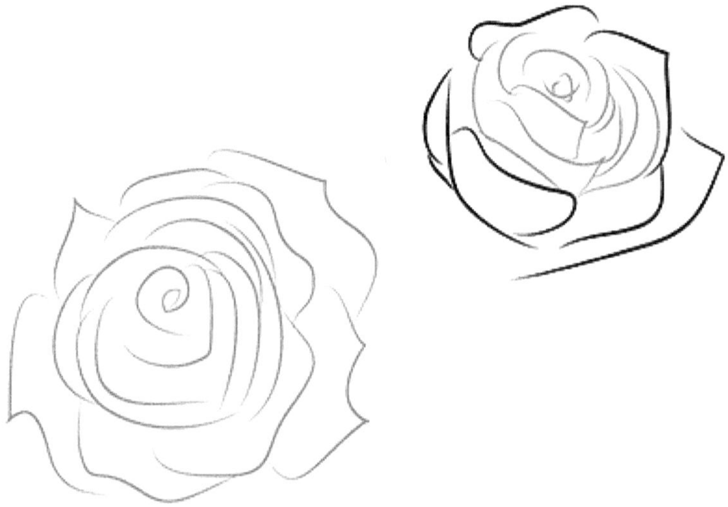

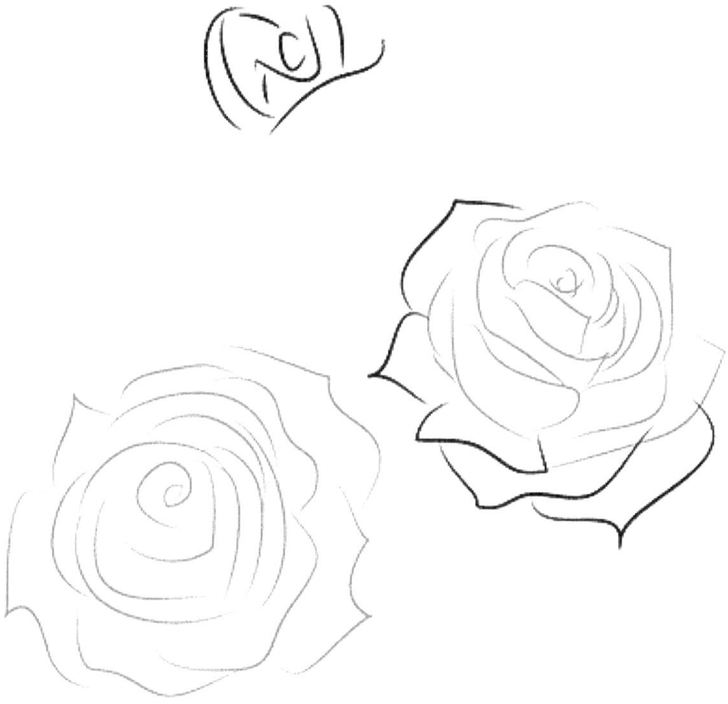

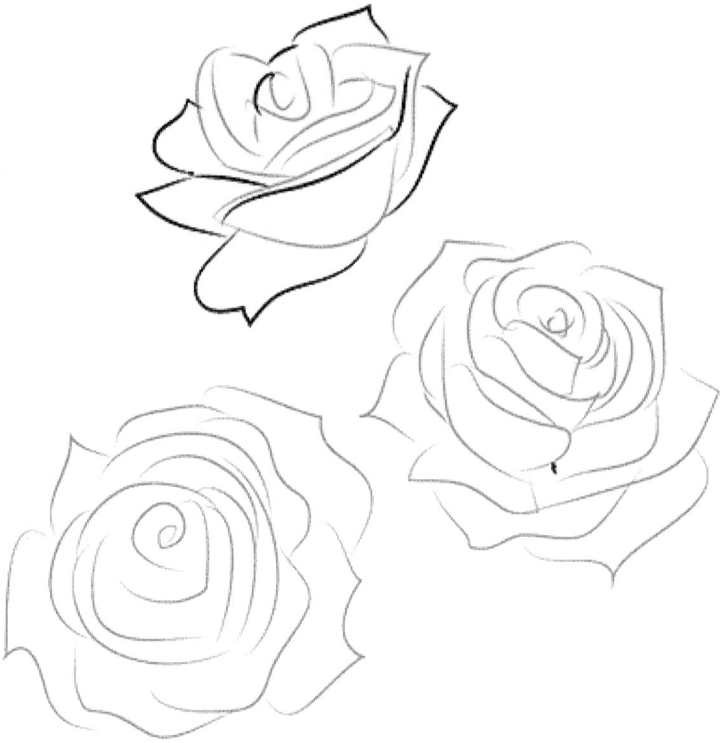

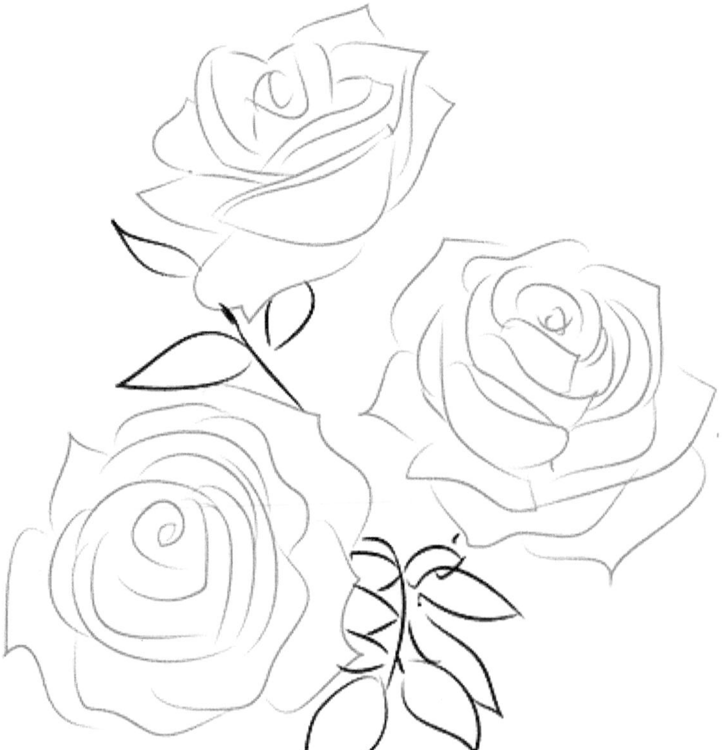

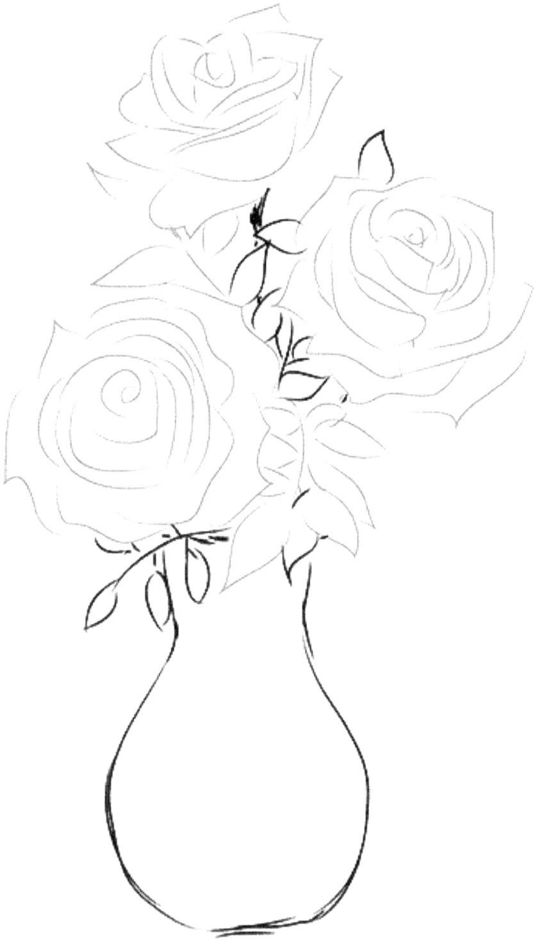

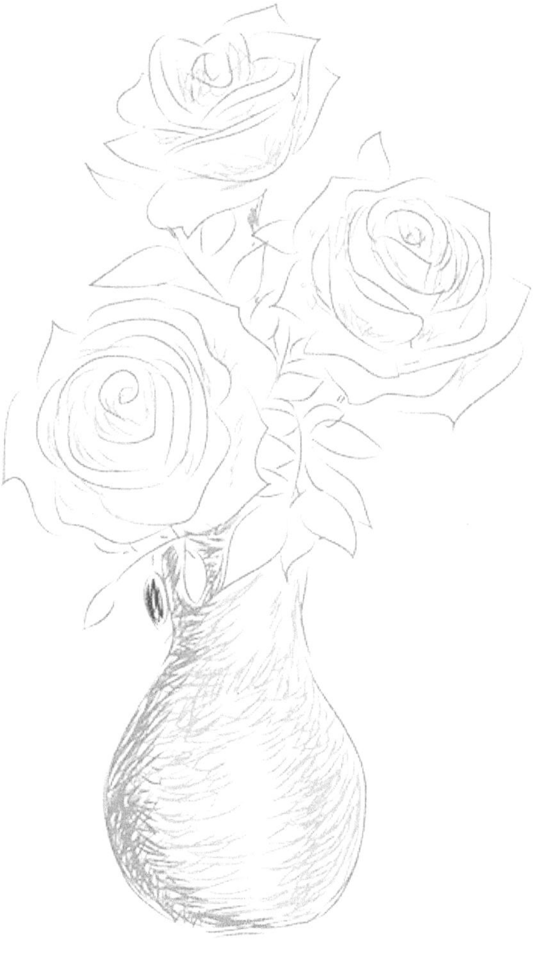

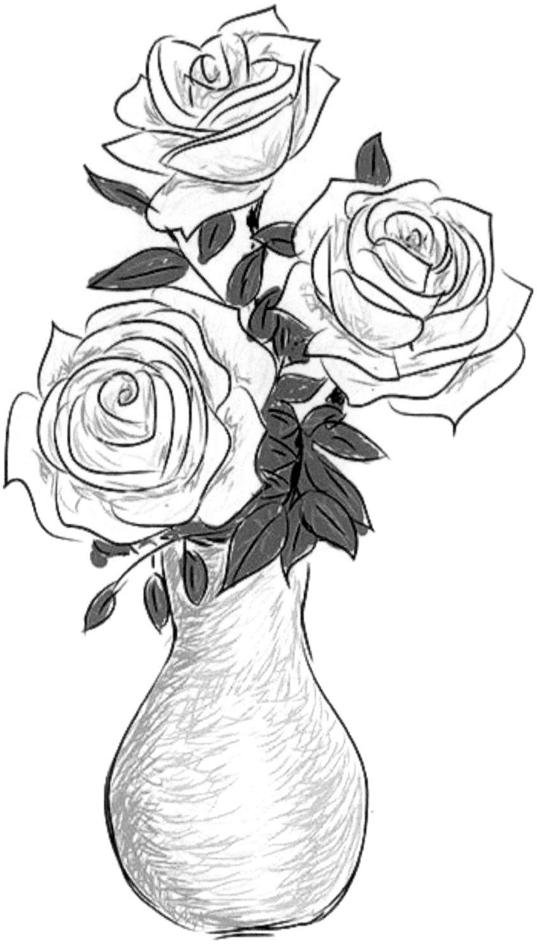

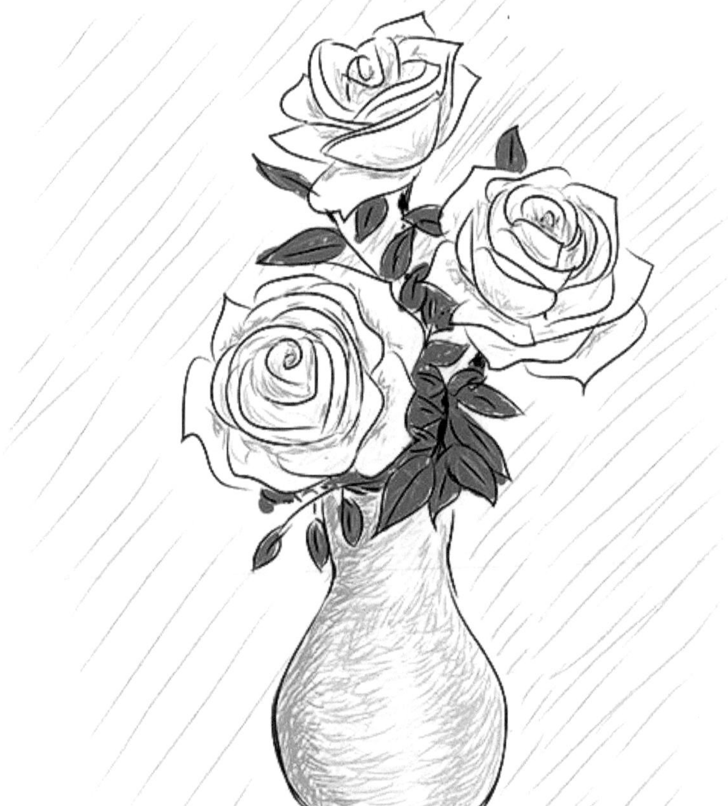

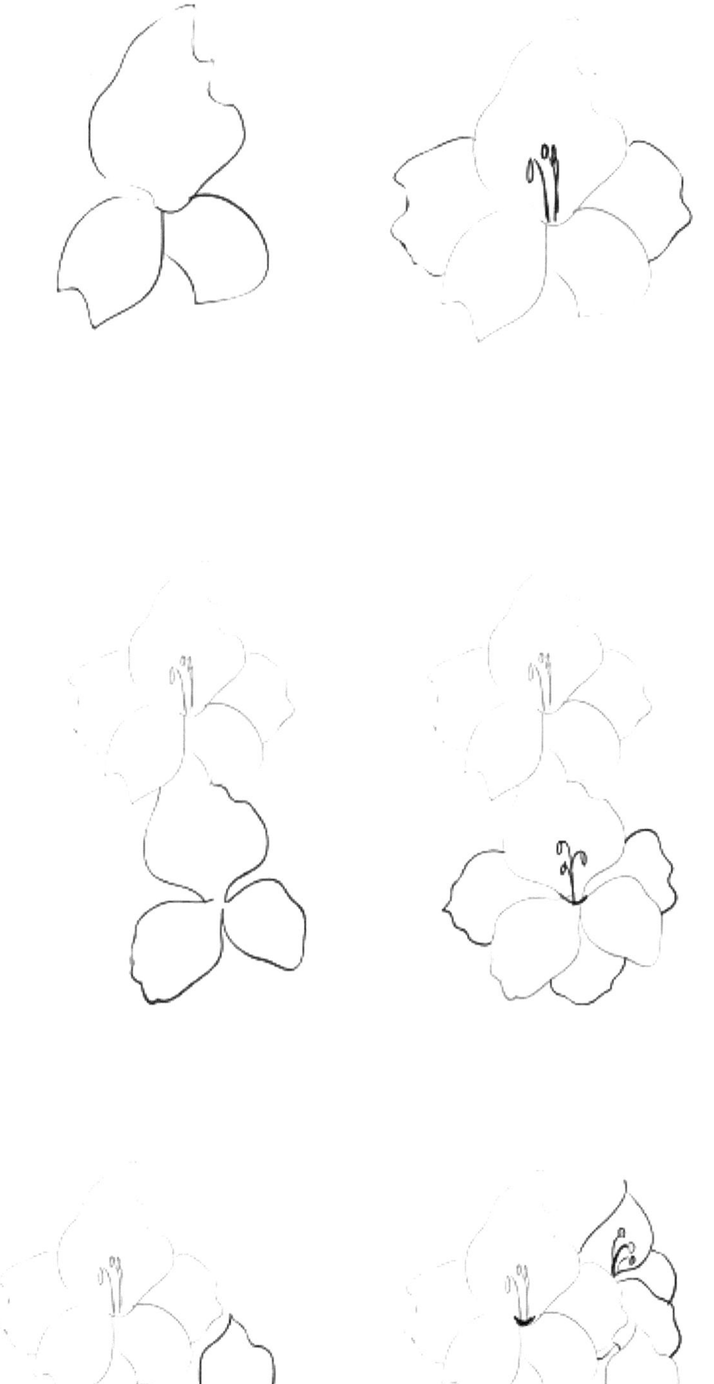

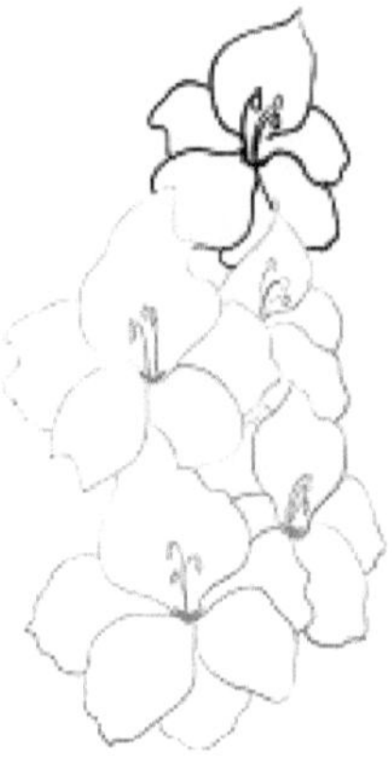
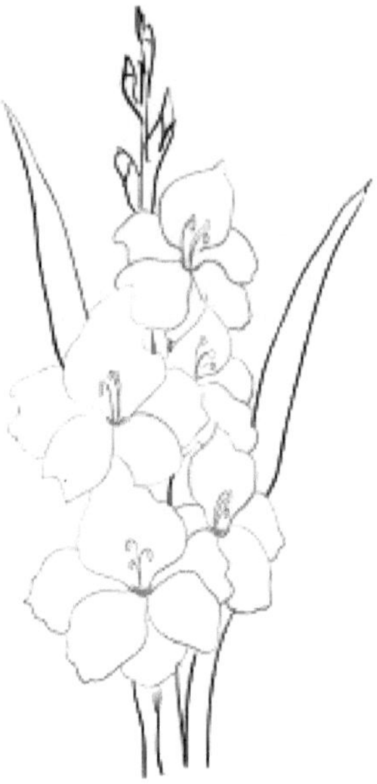
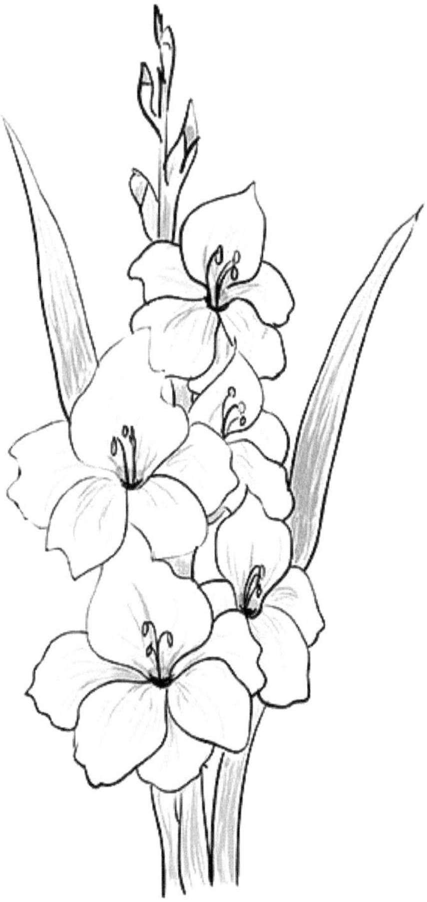

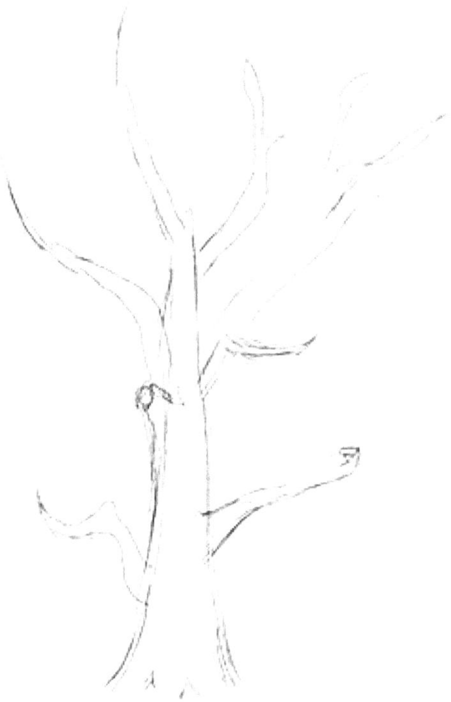

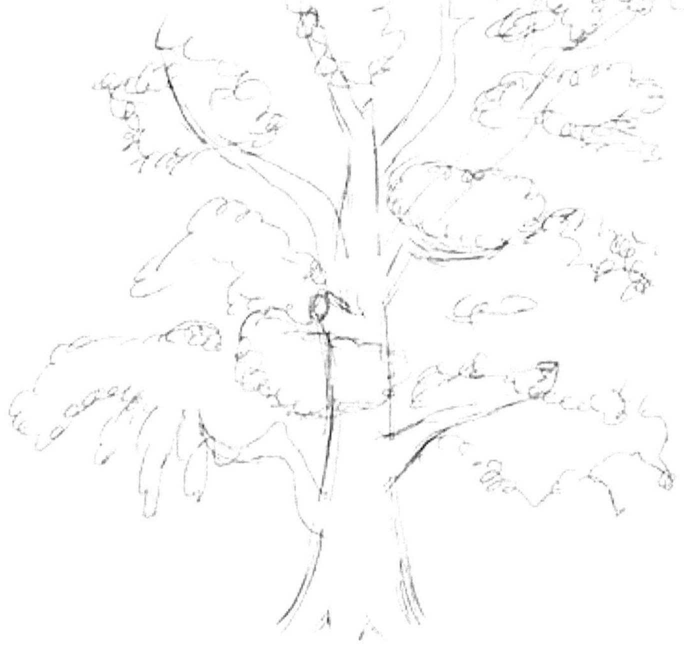

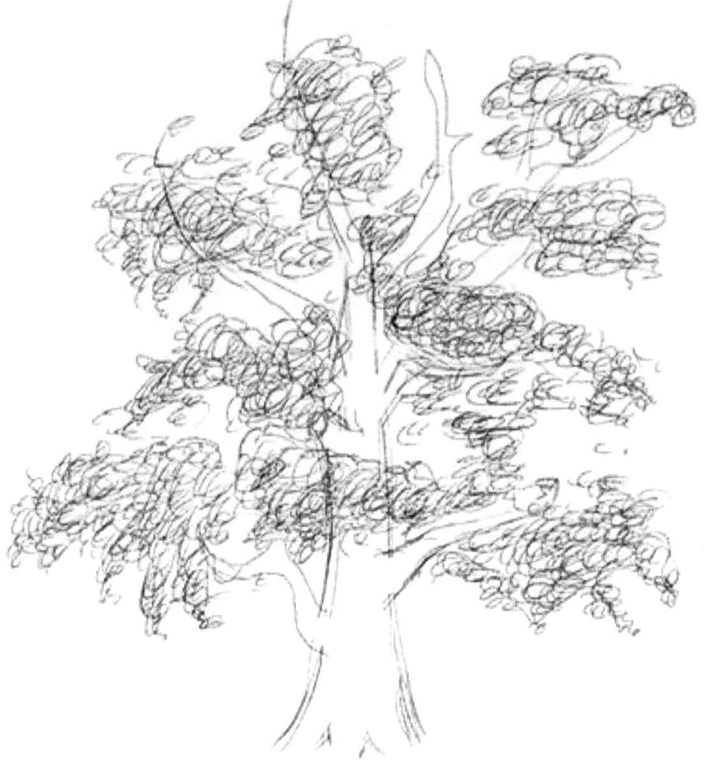

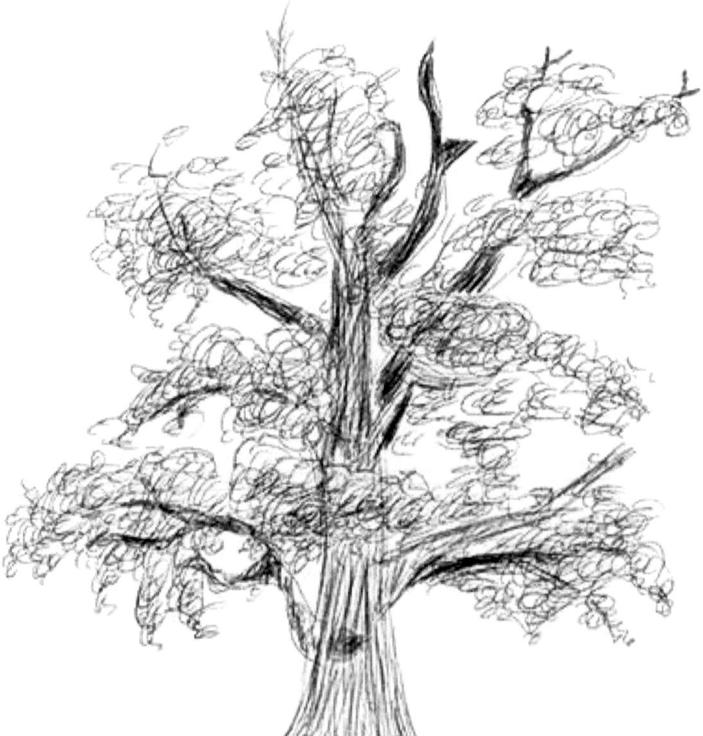

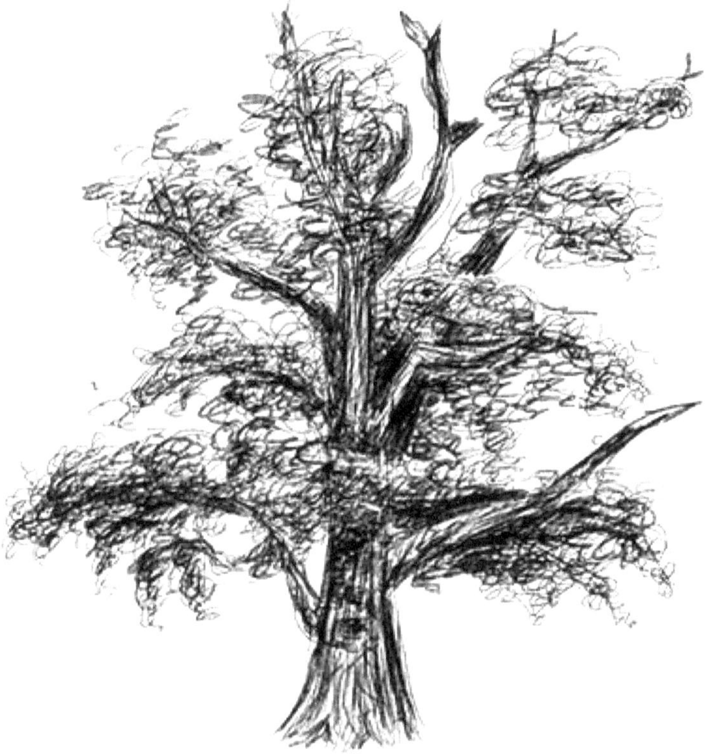

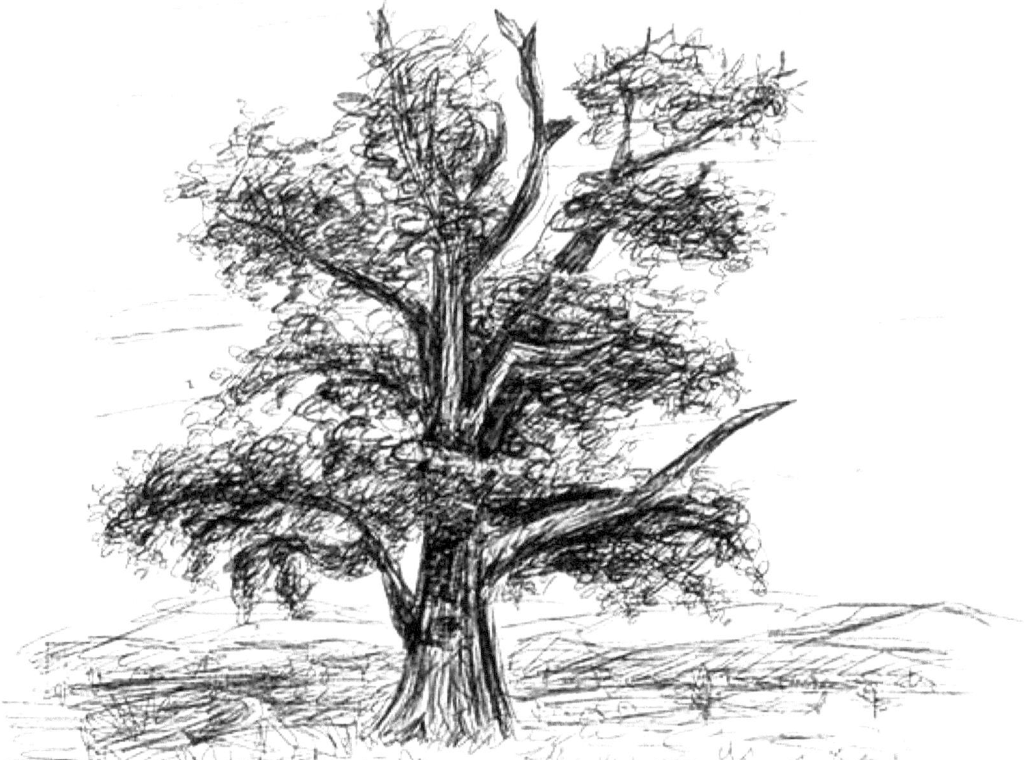

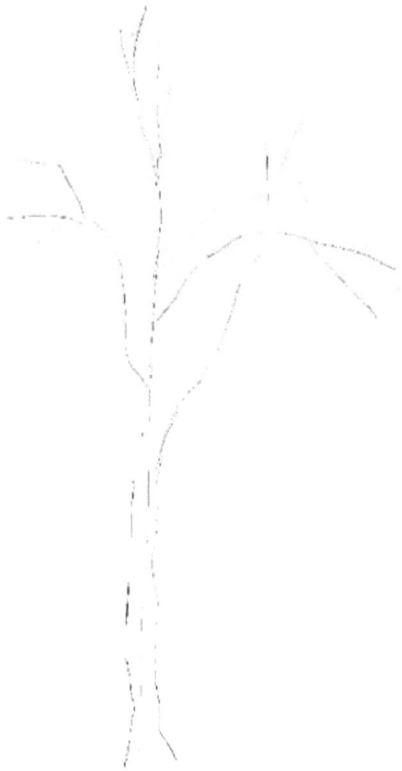

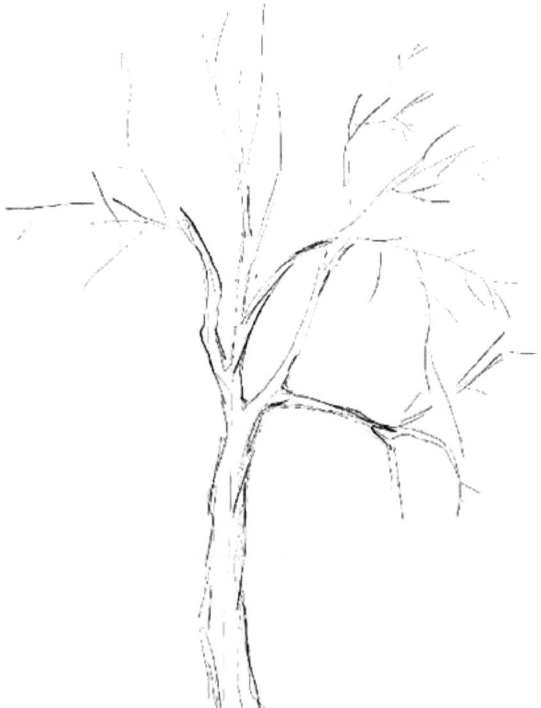

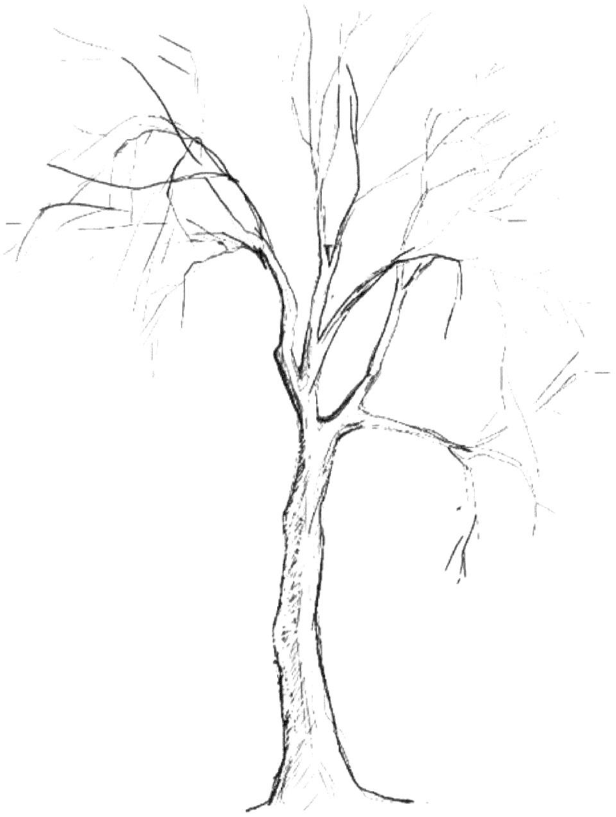

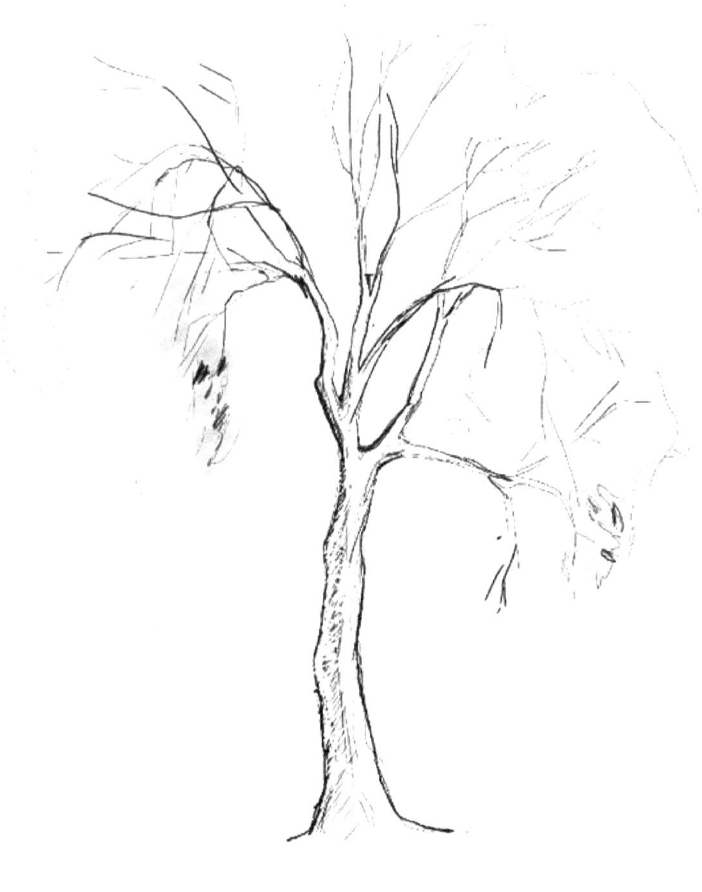

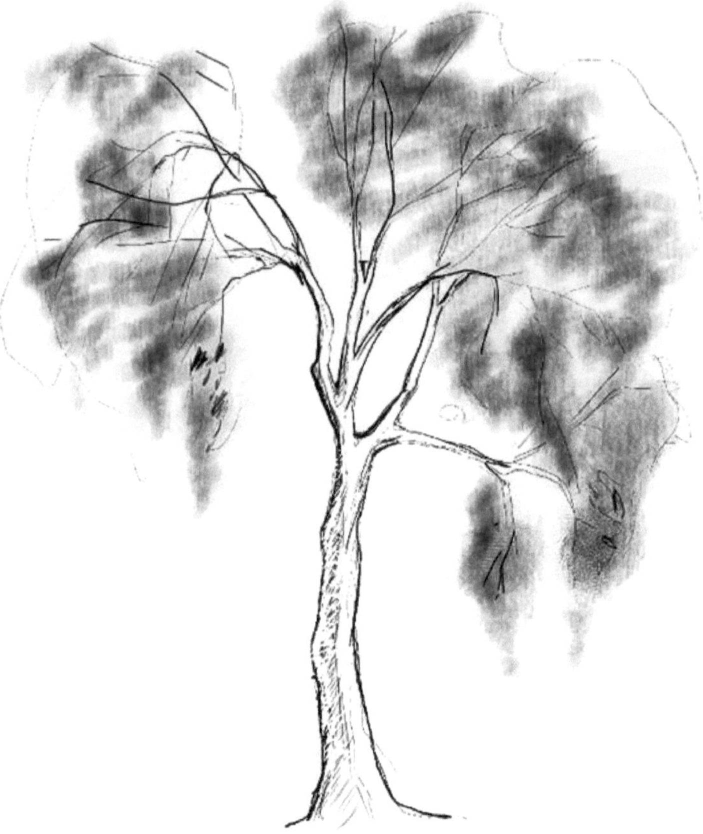

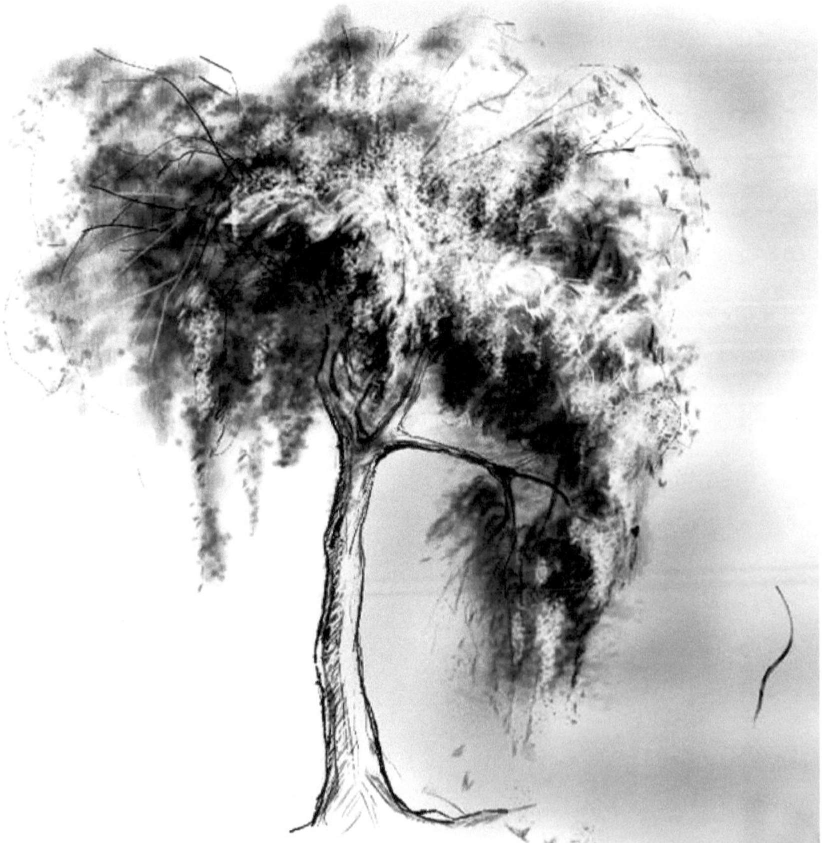

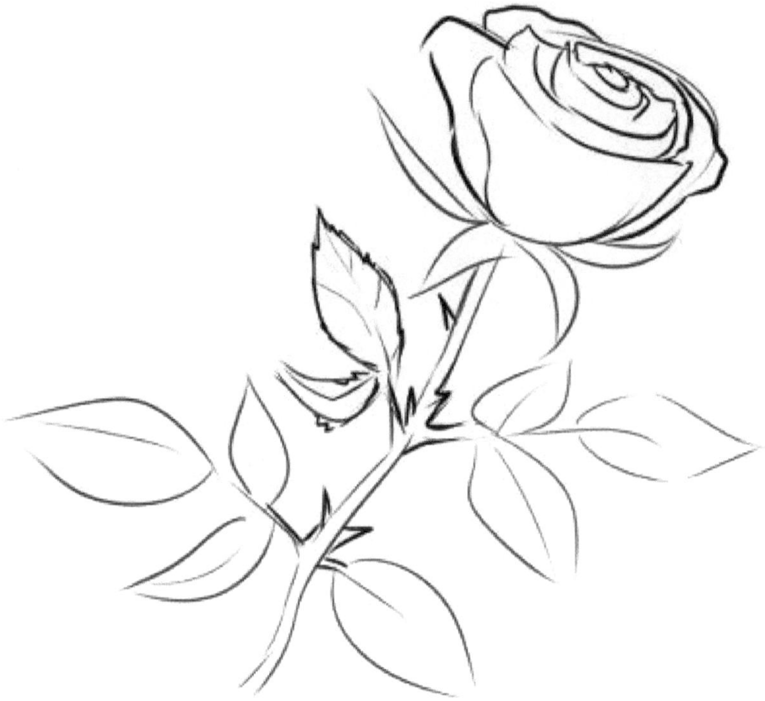

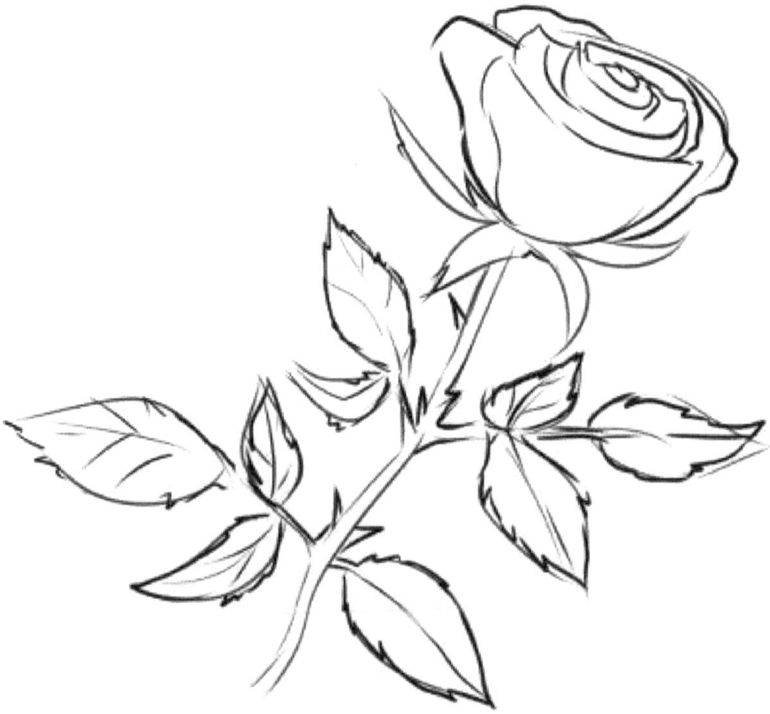

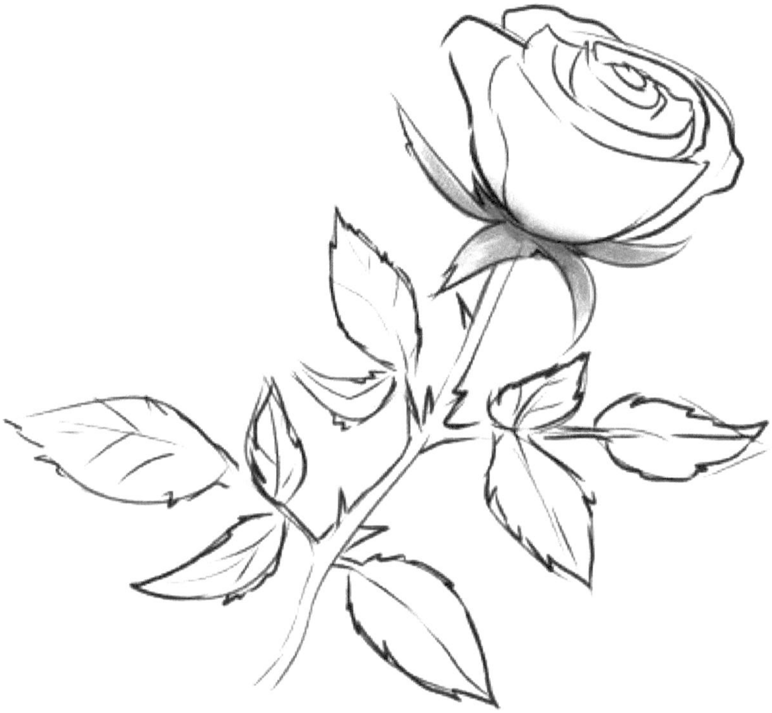

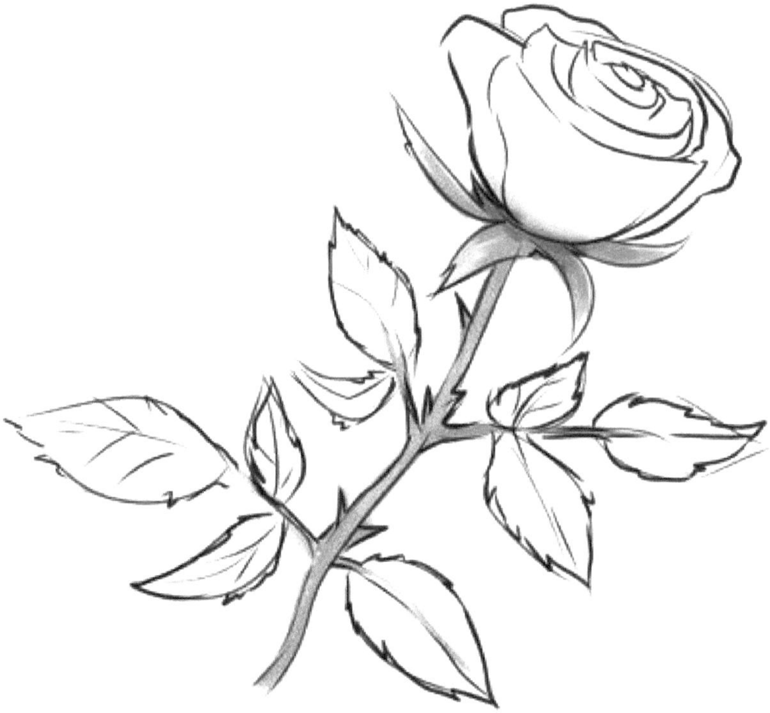

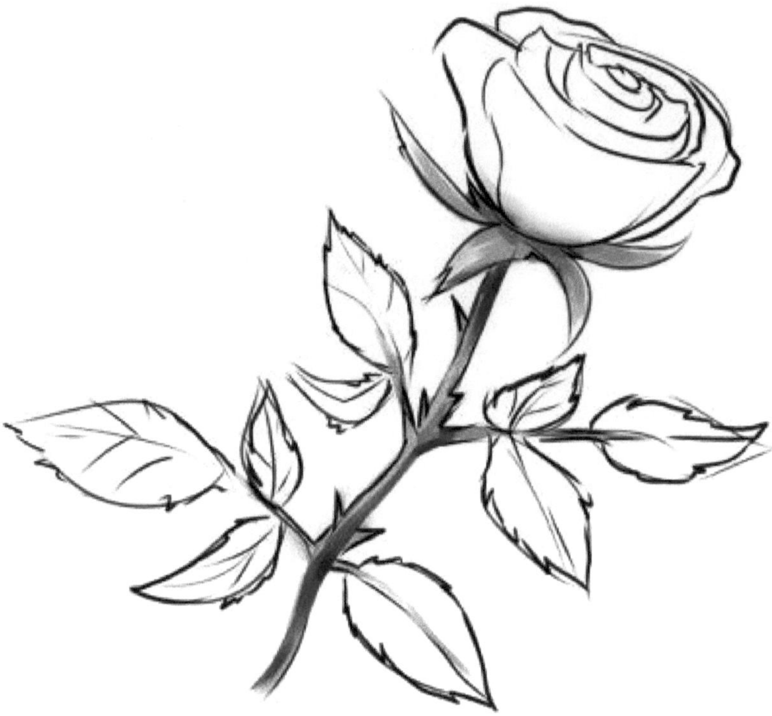
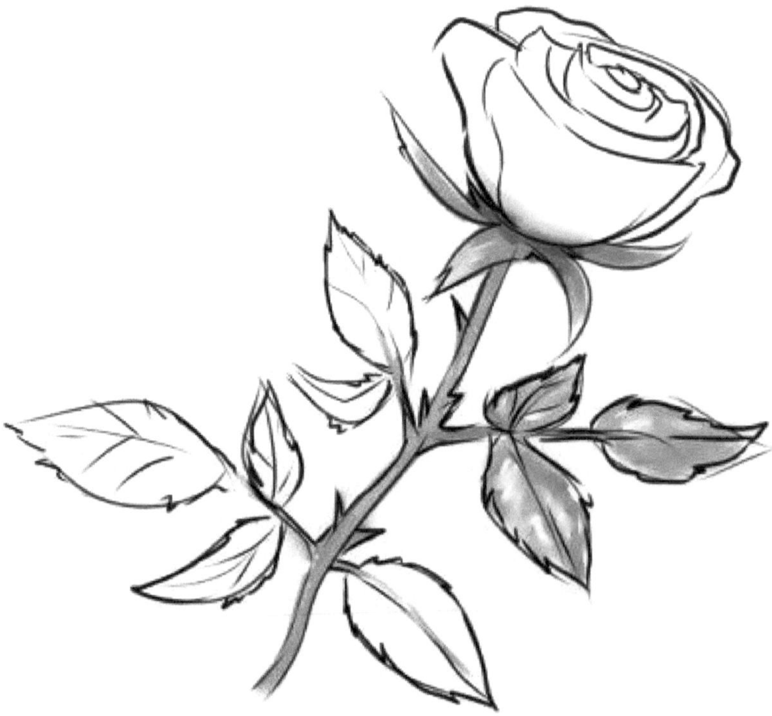

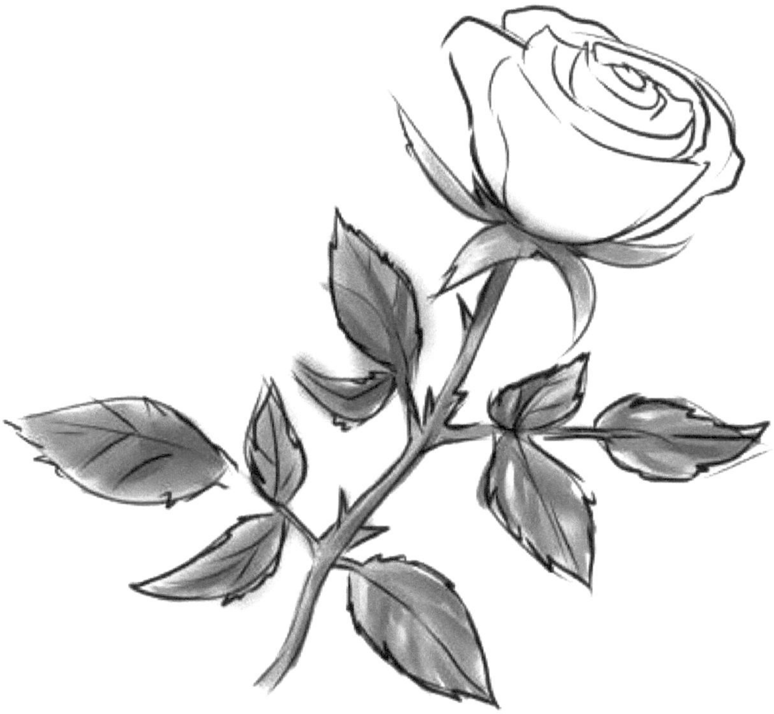

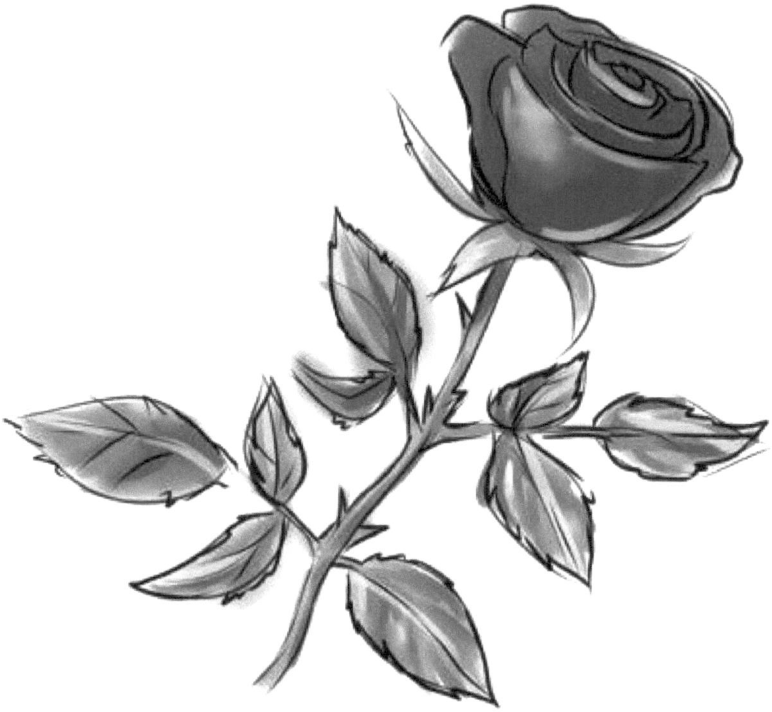

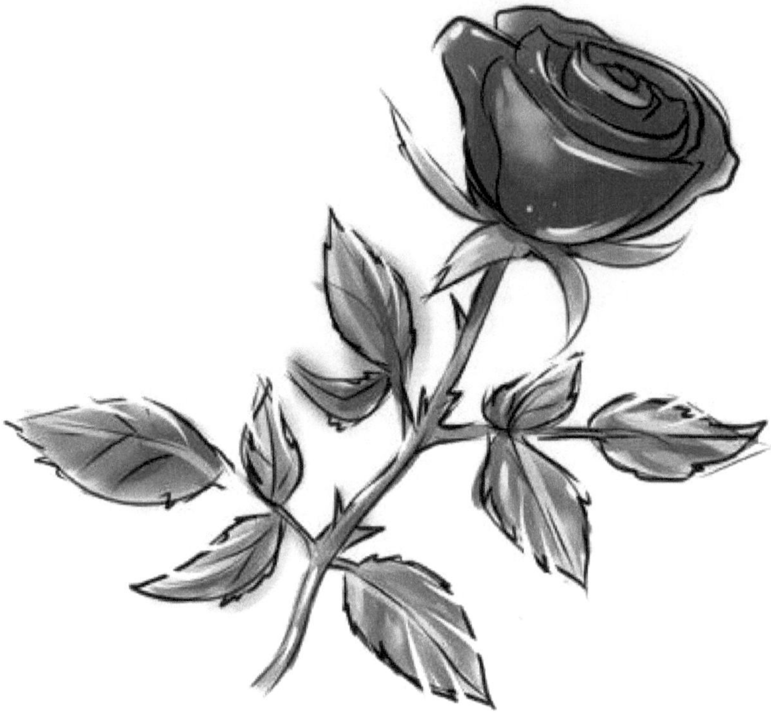

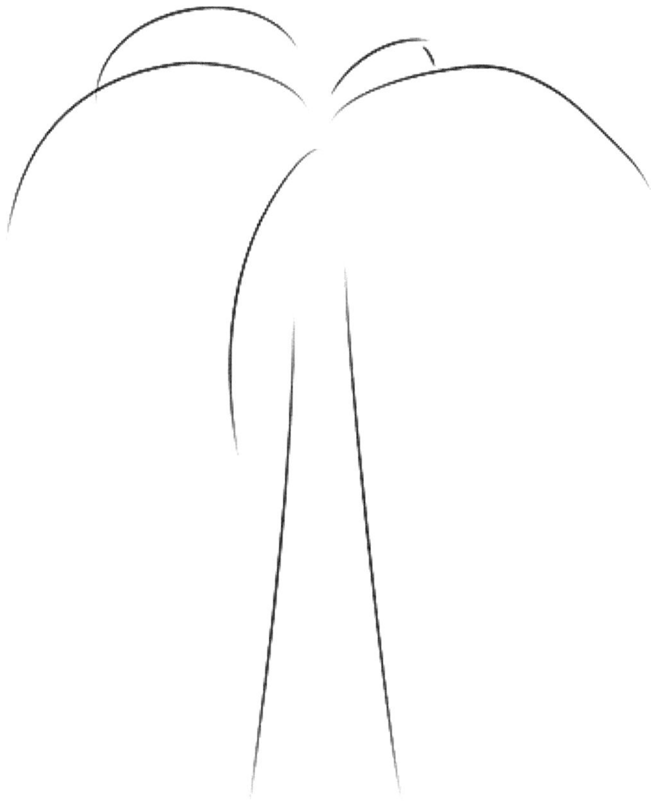

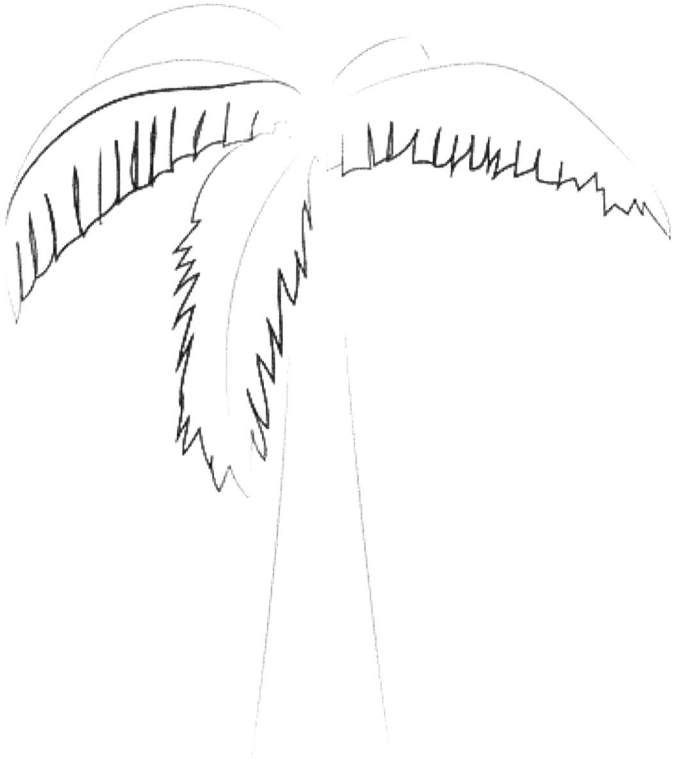

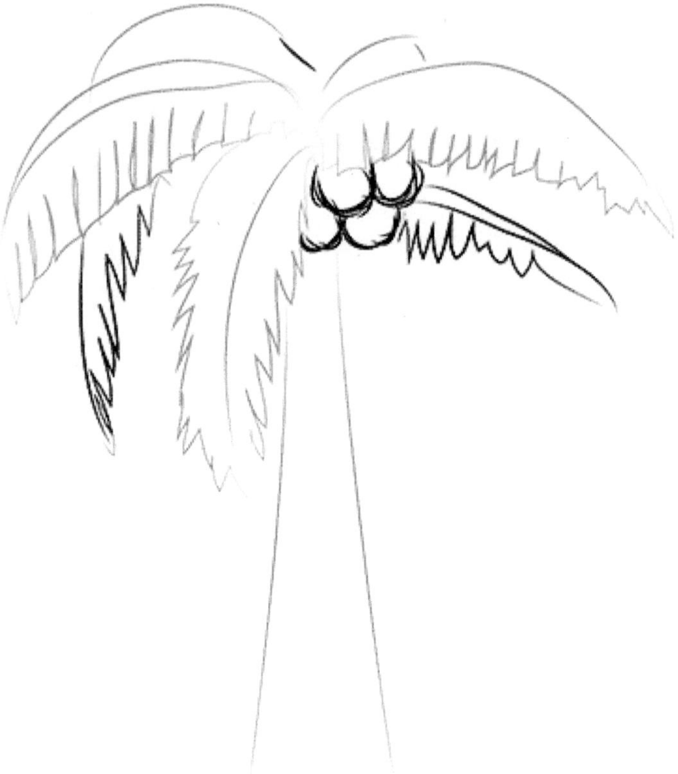

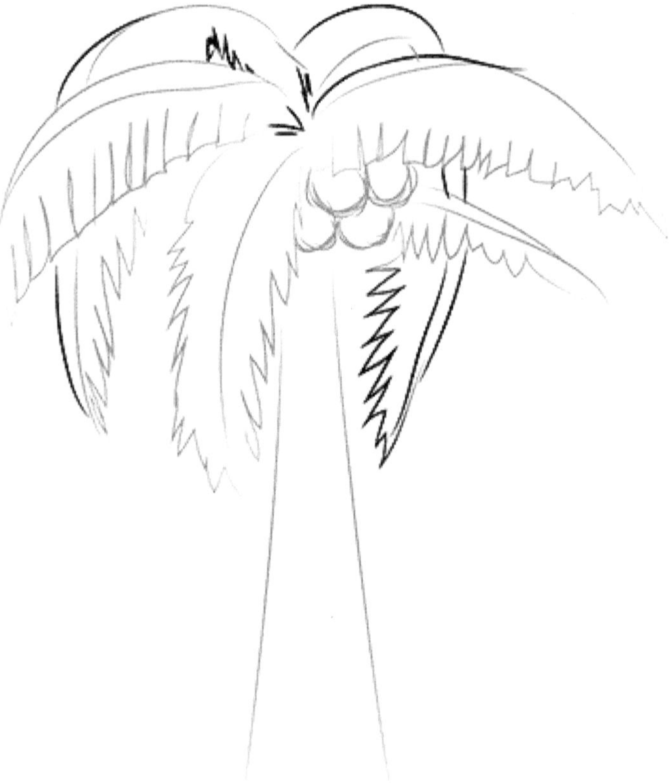

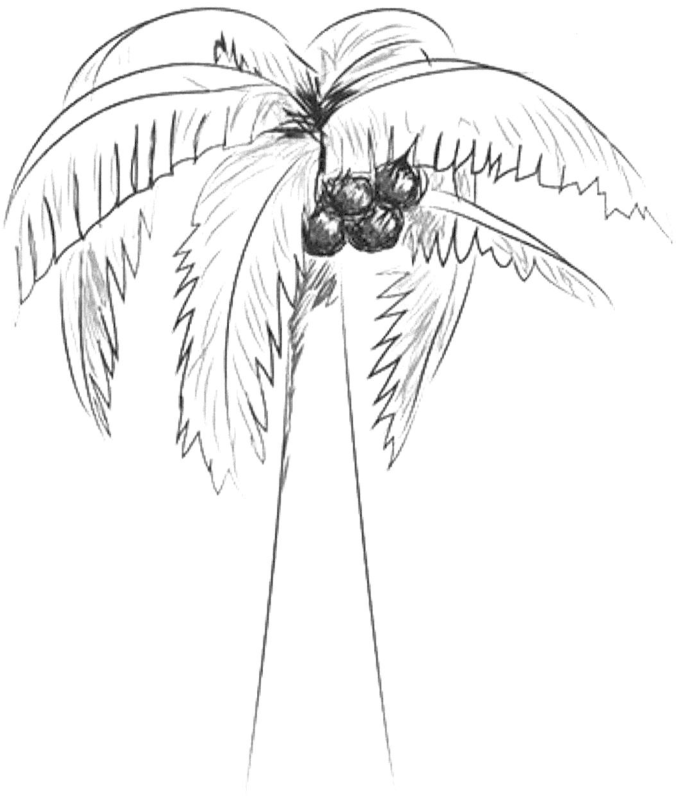

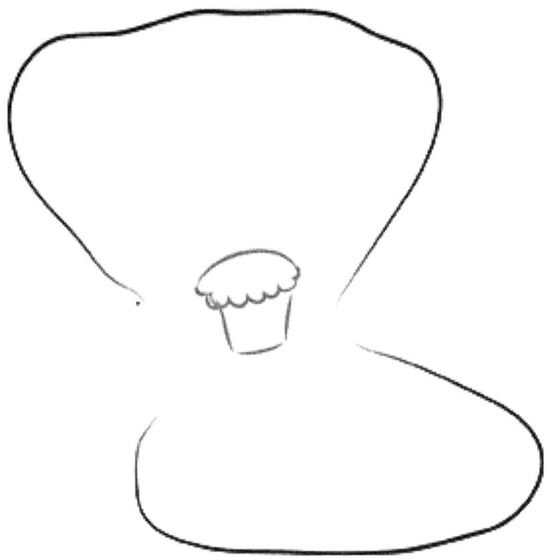
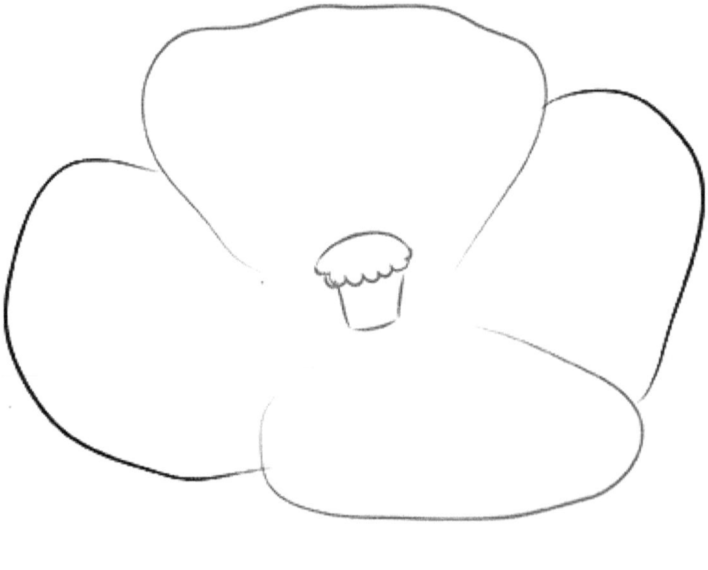

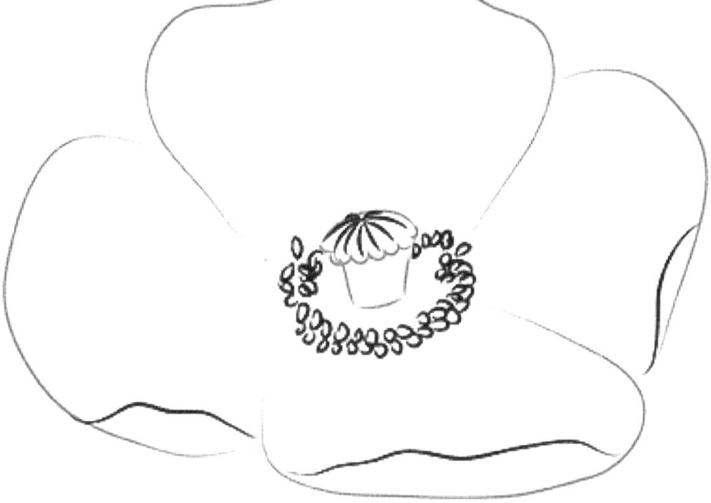

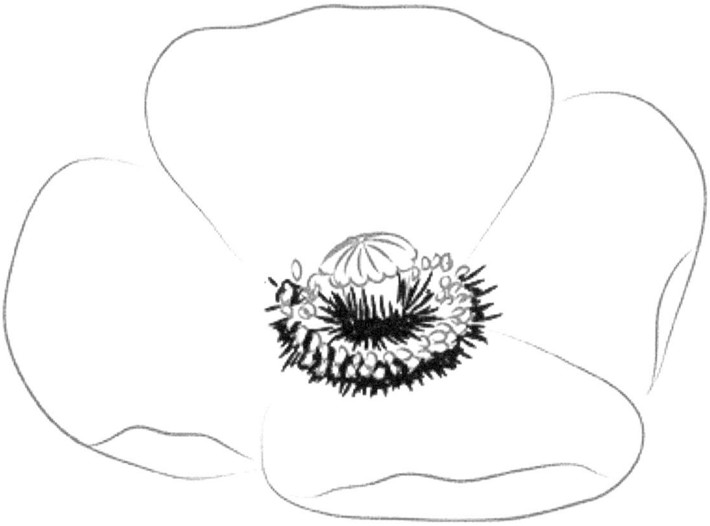

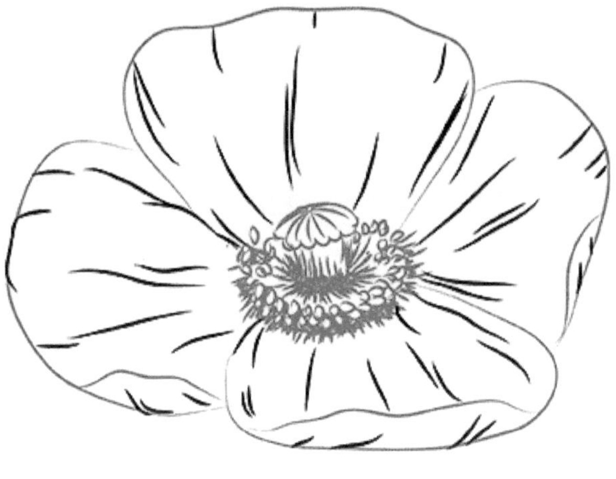
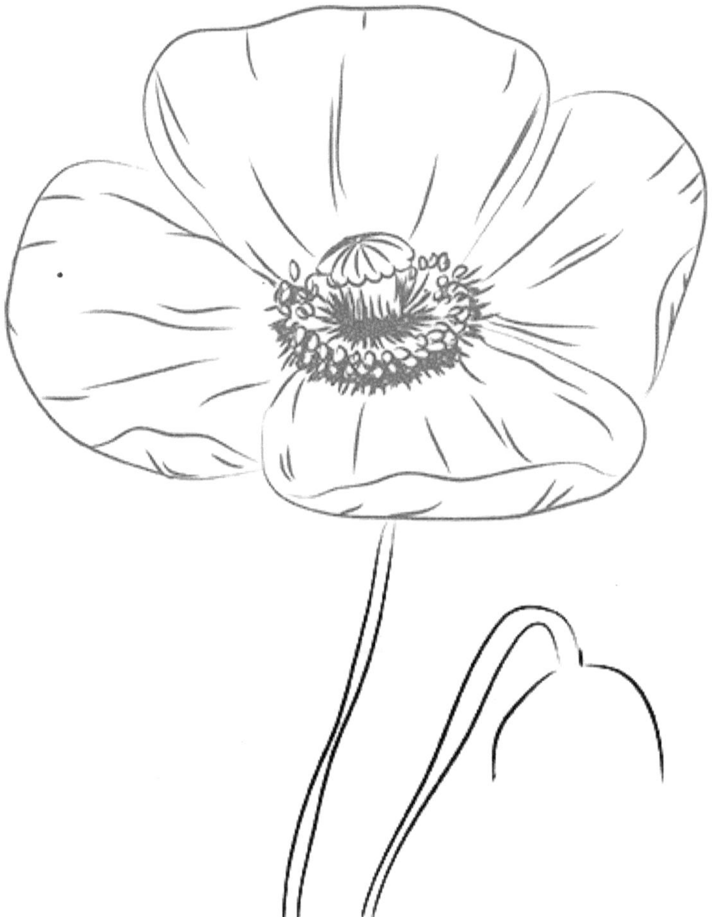

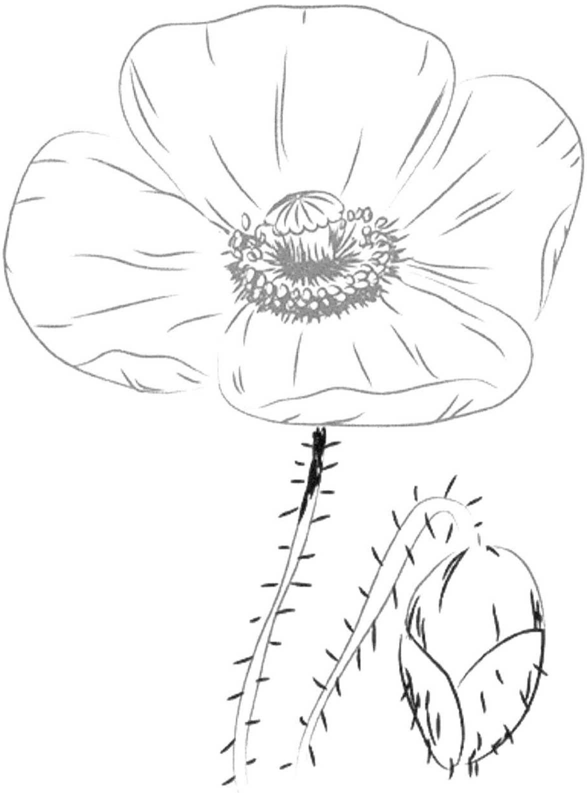

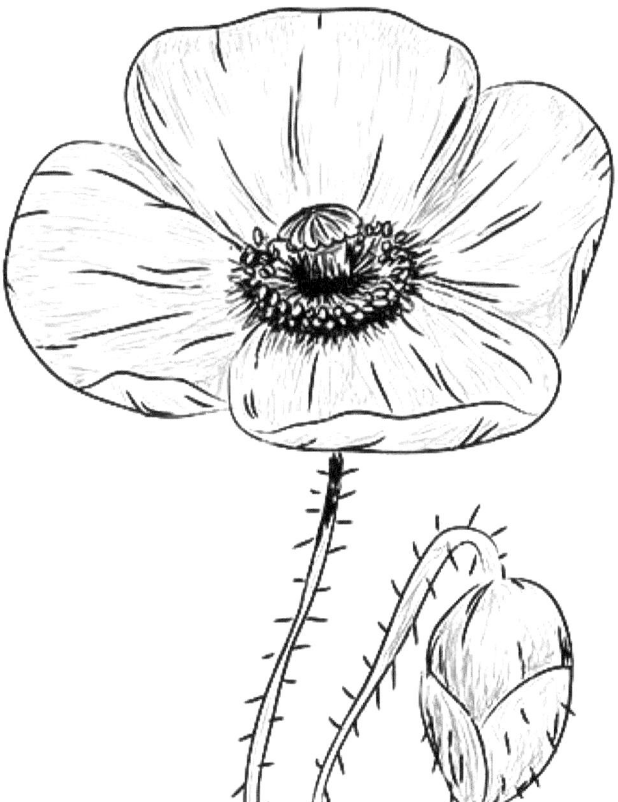

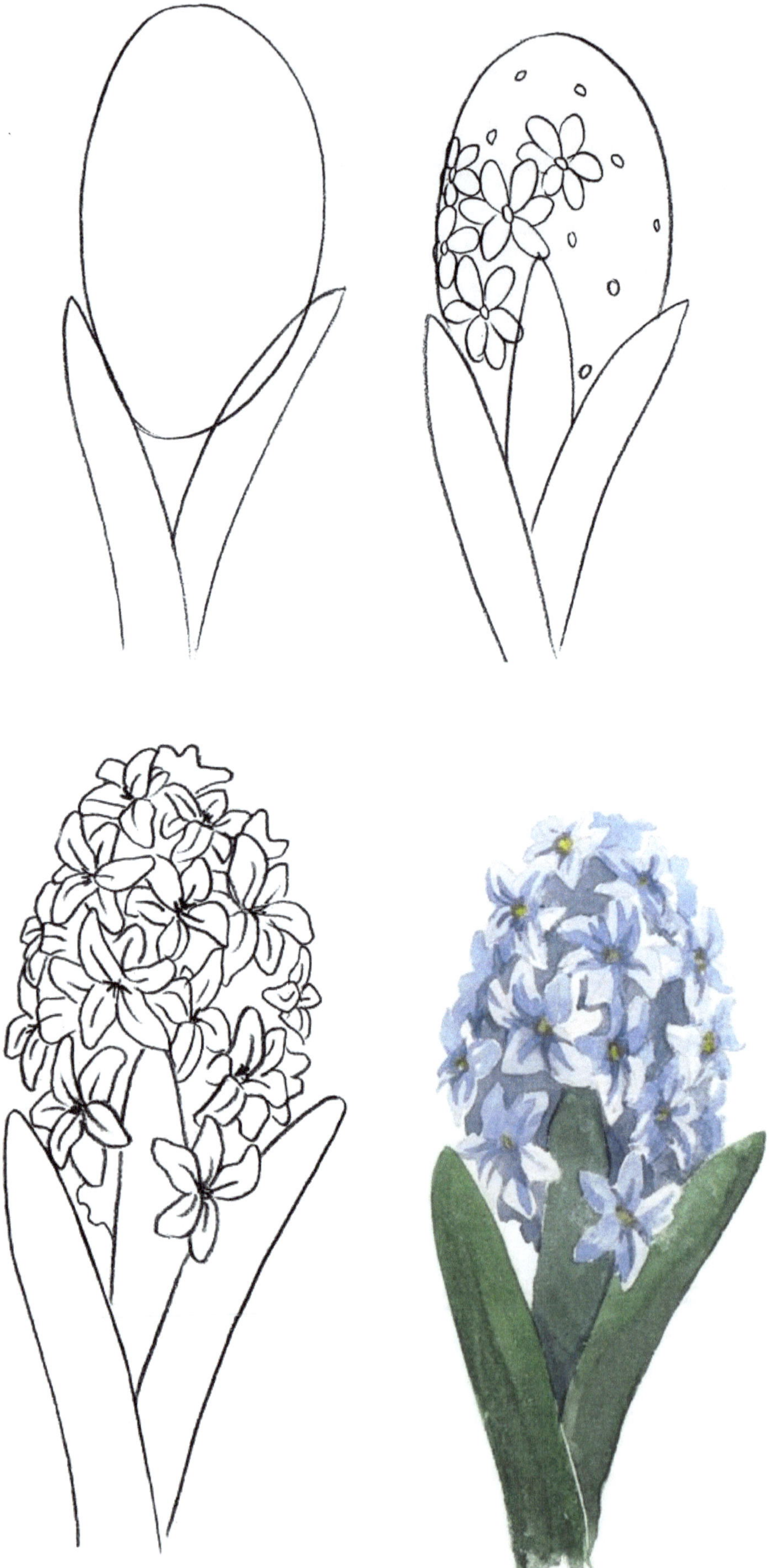

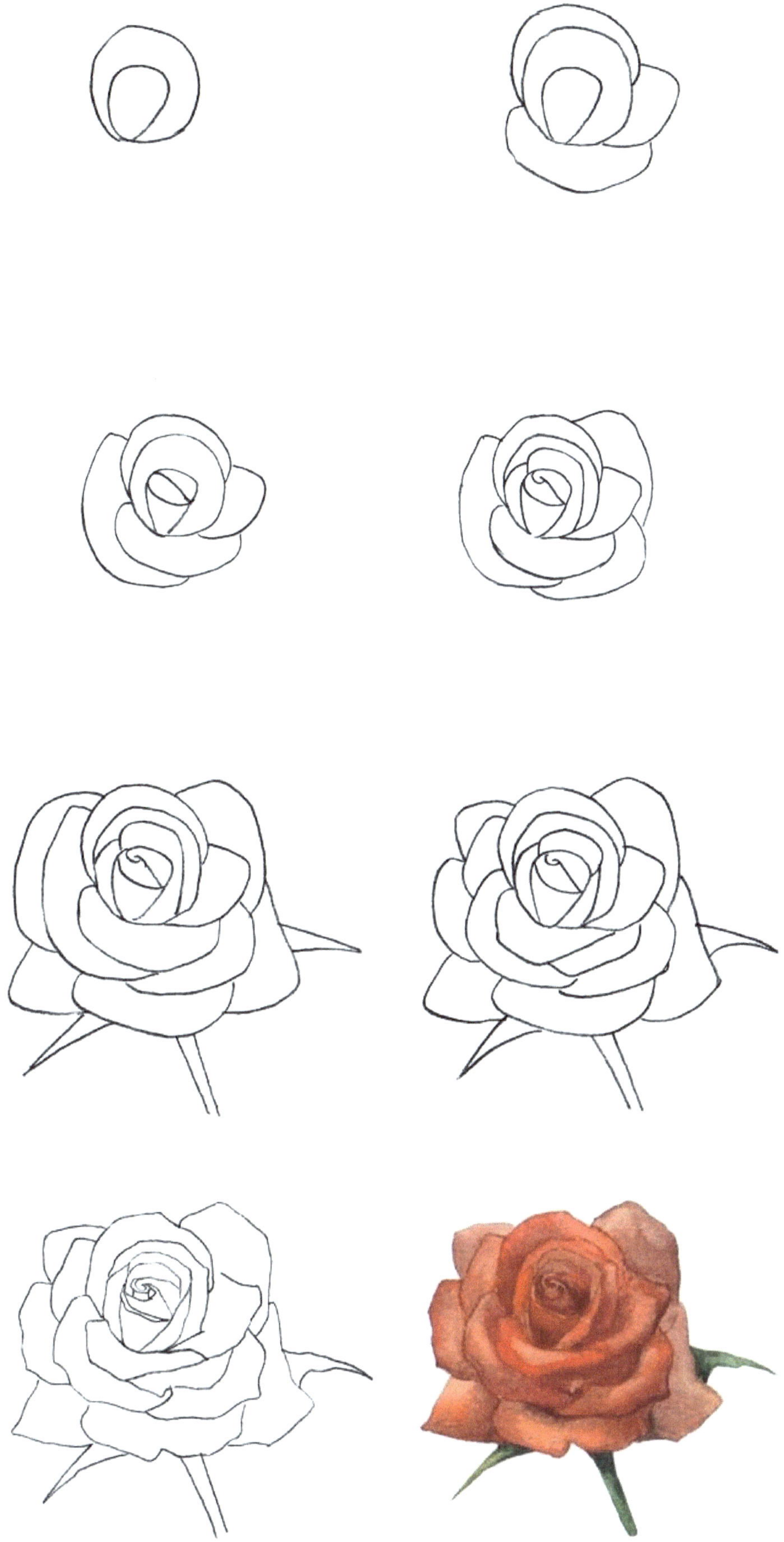

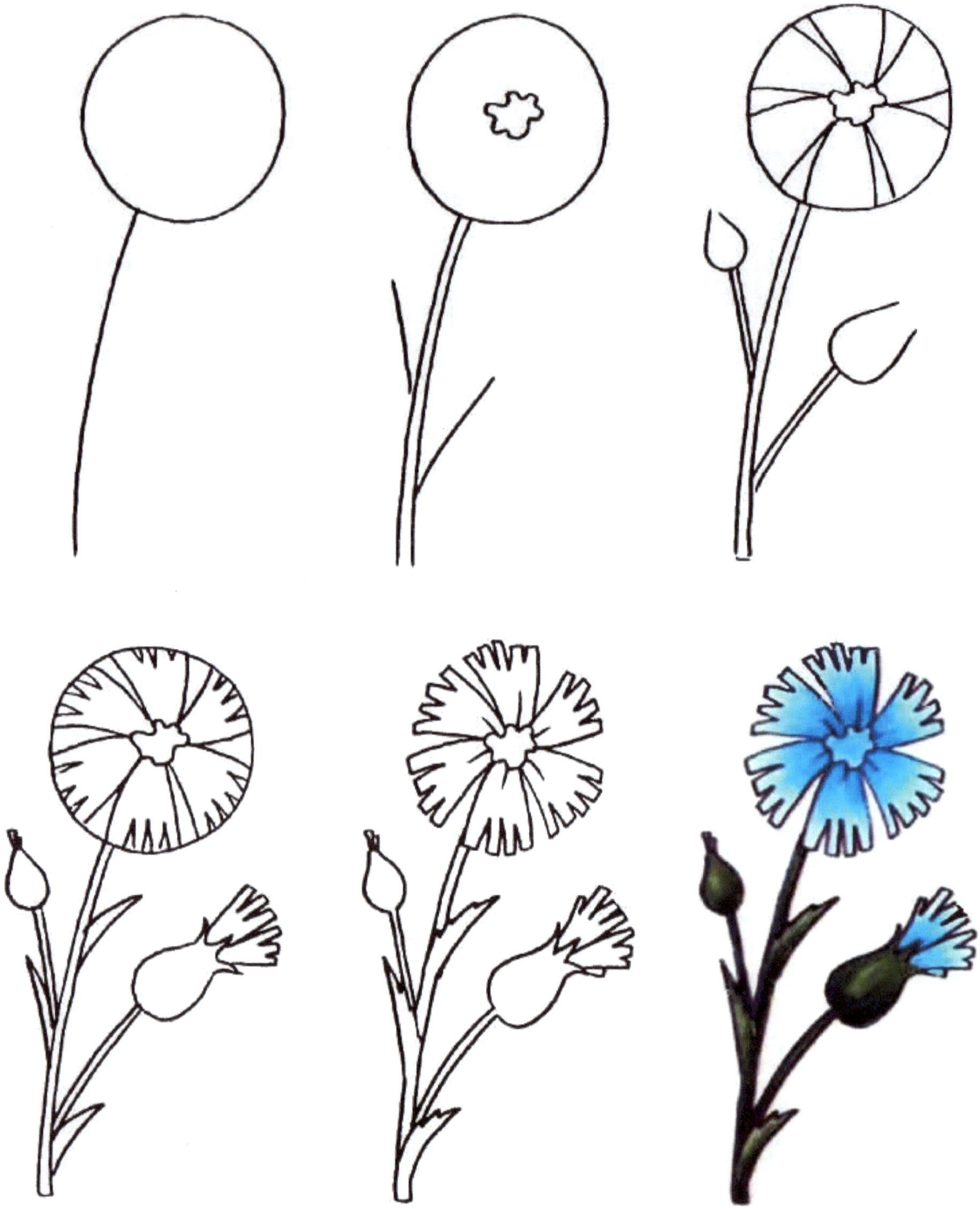

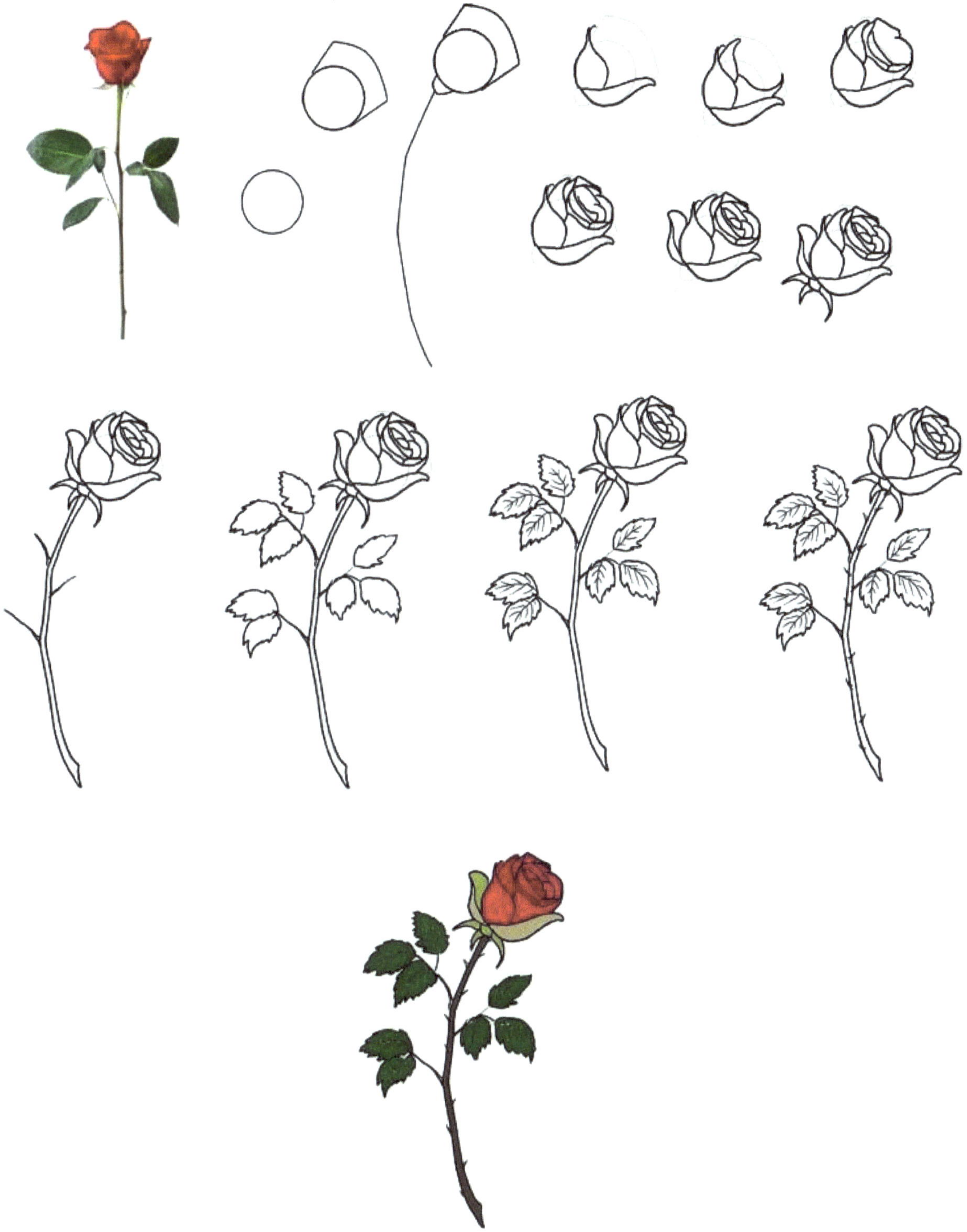

www.ingramcontent.com/pod-product-compliance
Lightning Source LLC
Chambersburg PA
CBHW040436220526
45473CB00004B/1455
* 9 7 9 8 6 1 5 6 4 2 4 4 9 *